"Theresa has done an excellent job of reviewing the working of remote teams from the lens of *culture*...a much needed perspective. The book has a nice combination of academic research and the stories of remote teams...making it an easy read. "

Amit Mittal, Vice President, Talent and Organizational
Development, Tetra Pak International SA

"Building global virtual teams across cultures that truly maximize the value of their diversity has never been more important for organizations. Theresa reveals the 'soft factors' that drive hard outcomes. Her blend of rigorous research and hands-on experience delivers invaluable insights, case-based examples and engaging tools - Team Taco Test anyone? - for leaders, HR experts and anyone committed to improving outcomes for business and their people."

Diane Moody, Vice President, Organizational Development &
Culture, Royal DSM

"Engaging and insightful. The conceptual argument is powerful and most of the authors' suggestions are practical and common sense. A recommendation for global leaders to facilitate cultural bridges to enable a diverse team to thrive."

Marlene de Koning, Director, Solutions Design EMEA-Workplace
Intelligence, Microsoft and President, Professional Women's
Network-Amsterdam

"This book is perfect for any virtual leader, and I know many leaders and teams in India who would benefit. Globalization is here to stay, and we all must develop to leverage the capabilities we have in different locations. Theresa has put a microscope to the virtual experience and this well-researched book is full of compelling ideas and practical solutions. The three ways culture impacts virtual teams is insightful and the four Leadership Levers are relevant for all leaders, but she has given the twist for virtual context. A must-read for anyone working virtually!"

> **Hari T.N.,** Co-author, *Saying No to Jugaad – The Making of Bigbasket*

"We've morphed into a virtual world now, in our work and our lives, with a myriad of new opportunities and challenges. Here Theresa has unpacked both, in a depth and detail extremely useful to any of us in cross-cultural and virtual arenas. This is a pioneering piece of work in how to navigate and use best practices to optimize our engagements in an expansive and novel horizon."

> **David Allen,** Author, *Getting Things Done: The Art of Stress-Free Productivity*

"I have been interested in the study of multicultural teams since my career began in HR almost 30 years ago. With the recent global pandemic, the need to do this successfully and virtually is even more critical than before. Theresa's consulting experience and research help uncover diagnosis, cultural understanding and competence, and what levers to pull to help ensure you not only maintain, but enhance your company's culture, collaboration and productivity."

> **Dan Domenech,** Chief Human Resources Officer, Hewlett Packard Enterprise Financial Services

THERESA SIGILLITO HOLLEMA

VIRTUAL TEAMS ACROSS CULTURES

Create Successful Teams
Around the World

To my husband Jelle Hollema

Contents

Contents

Foreword

As I answer emails, attend video calls, and call clients all over the world, I am amazed by the interconnectivity we share. When I first published *Riding the Wave of Culture* in 1993, virtual work included faxes and Fedex packages. People reading my book were meeting in person, relocating and flying. Now, the cultural diversity remains but the context is different. People are working virtually. With this book, Theresa has taken the next step and shown how the cultural diversity shows up in this new context.

As I speak with leaders around the world, they tell me that they are concerned with the environment and would support anything that leads to less flying and less travel in general. This all accelerated when the global Covid-19 virus attacked us all. Theresa, who was a consultant with our company for many years, has answered their needs with a book that uncovers the underlying complexity of global virtual teams and provides practical solutions for leaders with a global mindset.

Although the world is becoming more connected and more global, our research shows that cultural diversity remains strong. It has become even more complex because there is an emerging diversity of diversity with more women and younger generations joining the workforce. This means that developing cultural competence is more important than ever.

The timing of this book is important because leaders and teams have been working virtually across cultures, however with little guidance or advice on what that means. Theresa's work is research-based, which is valuable because it highlights the importance of practice within a sound theory.

Companies are keen to implement their global strategies, but they need the right culture and leaders. Leaders with a global mindset who recognize the dilemmas they face, often influenced by cultures, and engage in conversations that reconcile the dilemmas for innovation and performance.

Even though the medium is technology, these leaders don't want to only focus on tasks and agendas, they want to reconcile the humans with the technology. This book helps leaders on that reconciliation journey.

More than ever, global leaders and their teams need to develop cultural competence to succeed. Whether they get on a plane or sit behind a computer, culture is everywhere. From China, India, France or Mexico, leaders and talent are emerging across the world and the location no longer matters. But they still bring their cultural influences with them, in how they communicate and how they make decisions that influence project outcomes. But this book is also relevant for people who work from home. The world around them is getting more diverse as well. I am writing this in Amsterdam, knowing that more than 50% of my co-citizens in this wonderful city don't have Dutch parents.

This book, in other words, covers many needs for many people, amateurs and professional.

Enjoy reading it,
Fons Trompenaars

Introduction

Humans have been communicating across geographical distances for centuries through letters in the post or ticks of Morse code. Technological advancements in recent years have provided the platform for companies to expand their horizons, particularly in terms of who can collaborate together. In the 1980s, colleagues in the same company located in the US and Italy would work independently in their own countries and rarely interact with one another. Now they communicate daily, collaborate on common objectives and create groundbreaking solutions.

Businesses and other organizations rely on virtual teams to achieve their strategic goals, such as gaining global customers, assessing supply chains or developing regional innovation centers. They want the best people working on organization-wide challenges, irrespective of location. This means that people working together to achieve shared goals are doing so virtually and creating teams to leverage the power of the collective. Subsequently and fortuitously, these teams are often multicultural.

In spite of the growth in virtual teams, businesspeople have lagged behind in understanding how working virtually impacts feelings, thoughts and behavior of team members. Many people have approached working virtually by applying the same techniques as they did with their local colleagues.

As people worked virtually, they realized it was different, but they could not exactly determine why. They pointed out that they could not walk down the hall and ask a quick question, or they missed the casual conversations at the coffee machine, and this had an impact on how they felt about their remote colleagues.

The tools to communicate are ubiquitous. Hence, it is natural to assume that working virtually is simply learning how to use the communication and collaboration tools. Unfortunately, this common assumption limits people in realizing that working virtually is more than learning how to use the technology well. It is about learning what happens to us as colleagues when we are using technology.

More than Technology

The current landscape of virtual working offers opportunities for synergies, creativity, agility and responsiveness that previously could never have been considered possible. To achieve these benefits, organizations must rethink how people communicate, collaborate and lead.

To thrive in this interconnected, boundary-less environment, organizations must support their leaders and people to develop the competences to thrive. Leaders must release the inclination to micromanage and discover how they can empower and support remote employees. Team members must expand their capacity to communicate ideas, feelings and plans with colleagues in other countries while using technology effectively.

What I have seen consistently in my work as a cultural consultant to multinational corporations and teams around the world, and what is supported by decades of academic research, is that successful leadership of, and work in, virtual teams requires the recognition and acceptance of the differences between global virtual teams and co-located teams. From the simple act of using a phone to communicate to the challenge of giving feedback to a colleague in another country, the virtual nature of these interactions impacts the quality of the conversations. Therefore, to succeed in this virtual landscape, people must understand the context, evolve their mindset and develop the competences to lead and collaborate in an interconnected manner.

Three main competences are the foundation of this book:

1. Virtual Leadership: The ability to lead across time and space

2. Cultural Competence: The ability to succeed with people from other cultures
3. Virtual Competence: The ability to collaborate with remote colleagues

The paradox for people who work on multicultural virtual teams is that they need to develop cultural competence, but they must do so while remaining in their own country. Traditionally, people developed cultural competence by traveling to other countries and seeing and experiencing the different practices, norms and values. Now, however, more and more people are working across cultures and need to develop cultural competence, but are staying within their own environment. The person is no longer engaged with the physical cues like architecture, language or food that often signal a different culture. This means that organizations need to give additional support and attention to the development of cultural competence. The informal learning that comes from physically being there has decreased dramatically, whereas the interactions with culturally diverse colleagues has increased.

Frameworks and Models

Virtual Teams Across Cultures is written for leaders and teams to support the development of the mindset, knowledge and competences that are needed to succeed in the new virtual landscape. Having worked with leaders and teams across the globe, I have found that they appreciate having a moment to reflect on their experience and to understand the underlying dynamics that impact virtual teams. Through workshops, consulting projects and coaching conversations, they have the agency to respond in a new way that makes an impact on their teams. They are able to view their context and themselves with a new lens.

To support the development of the reader, I distinguish three categories of learning and application, each supported by a model or framework.

Category I - Virtual Team Context: The geographic distance, the cultural diversity and the use of technology have an impact on how leaders lead and how the teams collaborate. I have created the holistic CALDO model to distinguish the elements of a successful virtual team. The model focuses on the uniqueness of virtual teams and how this uniqueness impacts the other elements of a successful team.

Category II - Impact of Cultural Diversity: Cultural diversity impacts virtual teams in three distinct ways, which are described in this book. Team members need to understand the impact so that they can leverage the diversity rather than ignore it or drown in the differences. One key theme of this book is that virtual team leaders and members need to develop cultural competence.

Category III - Four Leadership Levers: Once the team leader understands the context and the impact of cultural diversity, he is ready to reflect on his leadership style and consider behaviors that will make a difference with the virtual team. This section is written to give the leader the agency to apply the ideas to their own very unique context.

My Three Pillars to Write this Book

When I began the process to create this book, I had the following question:

How does cultural diversity, geographic distance and technology impact how people think, feel and act when leading and working in virtual teams?

Over the past 15 years, I have witnessed firsthand as a cultural consultant how business professionals have been leading and working across cultures and how learning and development programs could make a difference, particularly in a team context. In 2013, I noticed that the requests from clients and the issues they were facing had changed. As companies reorganized to mirror global customers and supply chains, they identified that working across cultures was linked with working virtually. Cultural diversity and virtual work happened simultaneously, and often in the team context.

Consequently, I developed my consulting practice to support the leaders and teams to develop the competences and have the conversations that explore and embrace the new way of working and collaborating. My clients are multinationals who face the challenges and who apply the solutions discussed in this book.

My approach to the question above has three pillars. Firstly, through my consulting practice, I engaged with leaders and team members to deeply understand the challenges they faced and their plans for the future. My guiding star was to offer support for their organizations.

Secondly, I explored academia and the robust research on the topics of leadership, cultural diversity and virtual teams. I read more than 150 academic articles that look at the different angles in their research, and the insights and concepts that would apply to the business community. Many people may consider academia far removed from reality. Actually, this is changing. They are conducting more and more research in 'the wild,' meaning that they are examining companies and other organizations. I paid particular attention to this research, as the researchers had the qualifications and vigorous thought processes to deeply comprehend the topic.

Thirdly, I interviewed more than 40 business leaders who provided stories and examples of success. I have been impressed by those leaders who realized that their foundational purpose as a leader had not changed, but their mindset and behaviors did. During the interviews, they reflected on what worked and why it worked, and I have included some of their stories in this book.

Virtual Leaders

Having traveled the world and worked with leaders and teams, I have met many self-aware leaders who recognize their responsibility for leading and developing the team regardless of location. They want to support their teams, challenge and reframe their own thinking and that of their colleagues and achieve results that contribute meaningfully to the organization. As I shared the concepts and ideas, I noticed their moments of recognition as well as their excitement to make changes.

I have met many leaders who intuitively realize that they have to change their style for their virtual teams and organizations. They recognize that micromanagement is obsolete and entirely ineffective in the new landscape. Instead, successful virtual leaders develop their style to empower, clearly define deliverables and support the employees. They recognize that the complex questions the team faces are better addressed by the collective team, instead of the directive leader. These leaders work to create the connections between the team, and ensure that communication paths are well established so that the team can share, respond and collaborate to move forward.

I have also met many team leaders who notice an important phenomenon of virtual teams. The team members fill in the gap left by the physical absence of the team leader and take on more responsibility, make decisions on their own and support their colleagues. This opportunity is noticed by team leaders who have created the environment for this dynamic to happen.

Overview of the Book

This book is the culmination of the knowledge and insights gained as a consultant for global organizations, integrated with the models and concepts from robust academic research. The book is written for the business professional and contains concepts supported with stories based on true accounts. I took the liberty to change the names and combine stories so that the essence of the stories is clear for the reader.

The book is divided into two parts, based on the categories mentioned earlier. Part One is to set the context. I introduce the CALDO model as a holistic view of a team, and it is a guide for the rest of the book. In the context section, I have also included configuration, where the team members are located. This is an often-overlooked cause for some of the collaboration dynamics. I have created the 'Taco Sauce Test' to help leaders understand how some teams are spicier because of the location of the leader or the members.

Within Part One, are Chapters Two and Three about cultural diversity. After introducing the concepts of culture, I focus on the three distinct ways that cultural diversity impacts virtual teams. Within each of these distinctions, I share stories and examples that many readers will identify in their own situation. Although the reader may recognize the impact of cultural diversity of the first distinction (Within the Team) in diverse co-located teams, the other two distinctions are particularly for virtual teams. This section ends with ideas for teams to develop cultural competence virtually.

Part Two is titled Attitudes and Levers because these are the elements of the CALDO model. Chapter Four focuses on how the team members think and feel about each other, which I title the Attitudes and Beliefs. The chapter includes three sections: Trust, Psychological Safety and Shared Team Identity. Often called the 'soft topics' of a team, this chapter shows how critical they are for the success of a virtual team to achieve results, particularly if teams must be innovative or work in complex situations.

In the CALDO model, the Levers are the actions leaders and teams can implement in the virtual context. In Part Two, I have organized the potential actions into four Leadership Levers: Eliminate Uncertainty, Create the Team, Bring in the Humanity and Complete the Work. I detail each Lever in the context of the virtual team and explain why it is different than for a co-located team. Within the Lever Complete the Work, I focus on the technology the team uses and the effect on team efficiency.

Virtual Teams Across Cultures: Create Successful Teams Around the World is written for anyone who works virtually and wants to improve their ability to collaborate and succeed in this dynamic context. Although I reference academic research, this book is intended to be approachable and recognizable for anyone who works in virtual teams across cultures. The reader may want to jump to a certain topic that is of interest in the moment and that is possible with this book. The reader may want to consider, however, to read the configuration and cultural diversity parts of the book as a means to understand the context and purpose of the Levers.

In any case, I hope the readers feel they have more clarity and options in whichever way they approach this book. Through this book, I intend to contribute to the conversation on leadership, teams, cultural diversity and virtual work.

Part One: Context and Cultural Diversity

CHAPTER I

CALDO & Configuration

CALDO Model

How would I support a virtual team that is struggling? This is a question I often encounter in my consulting practice, and the answer is much more complex than a list of top 10 tips would imply. For instance, a colleague and I worked with a virtual team who were committed and driven to achieve their clear shared goals, but were burned out and overstressed. As we spoke with each team member, we realized the reasons were low levels of trust, type of leadership style and the communication tools they used. We designed an integrated program to support the virtual team that considered the whole of the team, and not only one aspect.

As I reflected on this and the many other virtual teams with whom I have worked, I saw the need to create a visual that shows the integration of the various components of a virtual team. For instance, how does leadership impact conflict resolution, how do shared goals impact trust, how does psychological safety impact creativity and how does all of this impact the team results? Given the virtual nature, I needed to add one more lens, which is to consider how cultural diversity and distance impact the entirety of the team.

For this reason, I created the CALDO model (Figure 1.1), a visual of the complete landscape of a virtual team.

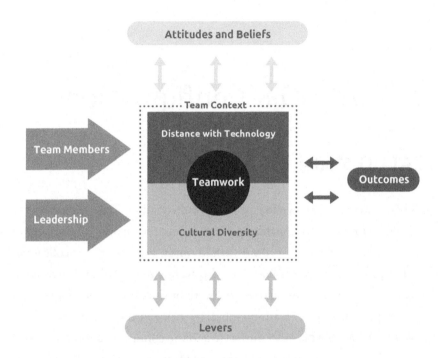

Figure 1.1 The CALDO Model

The Parts that Make the Whole

The CALDO model is a holistic model used to diagnose and evaluate how the global virtual team is functioning. As with all models or maps, it is a guide to trigger questions and conversations.

Before we delve into the core parts of the CALDO model, I want to first highlight all the double arrows that join the different elements. Team dynamics are not linear, but relational and exponential. For instance, as the team works together, the trust builds, and that helps the team to work better together, which in turn continues to impact the level of trust and so on.

The best place to start is in the middle of the model, with *cultural diversity* and *distance with technology*. These elements highlight the key reasons why global virtual teams are different from co-located teams. They are part of the context of the team, and this context has an impact on everything that happens within the team, including how team members think, feel and act amongst each other.

In the *team context* of the CALDO model is also where I include the team configuration, which can influence how well the team functions.

Once the context is understood, the next element is the atmosphere in the team, titled *attitudes and beliefs*, and is how the team members think and feel about each other and the team as a whole. *Attitudes and beliefs* include trust, psychological safety and shared team identity. Unfortunately these so-called 'soft topics' often go unnoticed in virtual teams. As much as technology enables virtual teams, subtle nuances of communication that would normally build trust are lost in emails and phone calls. The CALDO model includes these elements because they are so crucial for the success of a global team.

Two additional critical elements in the model are the roles of the team leaders and team members and their knowledge, attitude and competences in working with a global virtual team. Have they developed themselves to be effective within this working context?

The *levers* are the actions that the team leaders and members take to be successful. Once the dynamics of the virtual context are understood, leaders can apply the levers that are best for the team.

I have used the CALDO model to structure this book. By paying attention to the key elements identified in the CALDO model, teams will have the building blocks to help them to successfully reach their goals.

The CALDO Model in Action

Imagine a loosely constructed global team whose members only reluctantly share the minimum amount of information within the team. The team leader requests that the team members share their ideas and encourages them to contact each other more frequently, but to no avail. A typical band-aid approach would be to implement a KPI in each person's performance review and measure the amount of idea sharing. The leader could even implement a system in which team members are given points that they distribute to the other team members based on how much each person shared. The team member with the highest points would receive a reward, and the team member with the lowest would receive an online tutorial on sharing in a team.

The outcome would be a competitive game in which team members vote for their friends in the best case and question the judging criteria in the worst case. A more holistic approach with the CALDO model would look deeper at the cause of the sharing gap.

The CALDO solution would start with analyzing the context of the representative cultures involved and the team configuration: Are team members forming subgroups based on geographic location? Do they know each other? Do they understand how to communicate across cultures?

The next step would be to look at the team attitudes: What is the level of trust amongst the team members? Do they feel a shared team identity? Does the team experience psychological safety?

The team members and the team leader are also assessed: Do they have the knowledge, mindset and competence to work virtually? Do they effectively use the available communication tools?

Finally, what is being done to build the team and to strengthen the relationships? Does the team know the knowledge and capabilities of each team member? High performance teams use the CALDO model to investigate where the issues lie and what they can do to create a team culture of knowledge sharing, open communication and supportive cooperation.

The reader can use the CALDO model as a guide, and this book will fill in the details. The first place to begin is team configuration.

Team Configuration

Let's do a quick 'Taco Sauce Test' (Figure 1.2). Think of one of your virtual teams that you either lead or are a member.

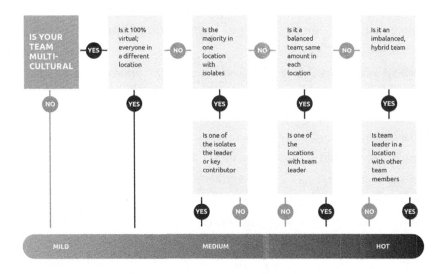

Figure 1.2 Taco Sauce Test for Team Configuration

The intensity meter indicates the challenge to collaboration simply due to configuration, the geographic location of team members. All virtual teams are not created equal, and team leaders need to manage and leverage the challenges and opportunities that configuration brings.

There are as many unique team configurations as there are stars in the sky. For instance, teams may be formed based on the location of their global customers. If the customer has three sites to which the company delivers, then the virtual team may consist of customer support people at the local offices of the three locations, with an additional person from the center of excellence at the corporate office.

Below are configuration types that apply to virtual teams in the same order as the Taco Sauce Test.

100% Remote Team: Everyone is in a different geographic location and all communication is dependent on available technologies, be it telephone, video, chat, etc. Generally, everyone has the same situation.

Hybrid Team: Hybrid teams appear when at least one location has more than one person. For instance, a configuration of 6-1, 3-3-2, or 4-2-1-1. Hybrid configurations are the most challenging, which seems paradoxical because having multiple team members in one location would seem like a benefit. The hybrid configuration of 3-3-2, for example, would mean that each team member has a local colleague with whom to converse in the local language, to socialize with over lunch and to spontaneously share information. Yet these innocent configurations can cause problems for cross-location collaboration.[1]

The challenge for hybrid teams is the establishment of subgroups that form at each location. These subgroups are often strengthened when local colleagues speak with each other and reinforce the 'us vs them' mentality. The section Between the Locations explains in detail why hybrid teams are unique and how teams can build the bridges between locations.

Following are various types of hybrid teams.

Isolates: The core of the team is in one location and one or more persons are each in their own locations. Anyone who has ever been an isolate knows how hard it is to get the attention of the core, or to be included in decisions, especially those made by the core during lunch or at the coffee machine.

There are, however, two instances when this configuration benefits the team, and this is when the isolate is either a team leader or someone critical to the success of the team. The need to involve these key people propels the team to develop an inclusive process for communication and documentation. Also, these critical isolates can be a counterweight to any groupthink that may be forming.

The Isolate Team Leader

Sometimes what may seem like a disadvantage of a team configuration can turn into an advantage. Over the years, I have followed the career of Tony, Head of E-Commerce at a major Nordic bank, a company that introduced virtual work years ago and now consider it part of their normal way of working. Tony, who is located in Denmark, was either a member or a leader of a hybrid virtual team until he was promoted to lead a team where everyone except Tony was located in Poland. Tony reflected on his experience as an isolate leader.

"For me, the challenge was how can I be close to the team even though I am not sitting there together with them. In the beginning, I had some concerns about this setup. I was afraid that I would be left out. I noticed that the team does not always include me in everything. They solve a lot of issues themselves. If the issues are brought to me, it is because they are facing some challenges they want to discuss, or they have made a decision amongst themselves and they would like to tell me."

Tony continued his description of the team dynamic, including how well this type of configuration can function: "If they can solve *the operational issues, and they discuss it between themselves, they typically don't inform me. And I am fine with that because it means that they are taking ownership and responsibility. They also told me that they like this trust from my side, to solve issues by themselves first. In the beginning I was wondering if I am losing something by not being involved, but now I do not have that feeling. Now when they come up with a question, they want to discuss it with me so that I can give them some direction. Based on my knowledge and experience, I can guide them or challenge their thinking. They have told me that they like that and appreciate it. I don't feel like I am left out."*

Tony's story shows how a team configuration has advantages when compared to co-location, specifically the development and empowerment of the team members in the absence of the leader's physical presence. His supportive leadership style built the trust and connections for the team to thrive.

Balanced Team: This configuration contains an equal number of people in multiple locations. It gives the impression of a power balance until we consider the benefits of certain locations, such as who is in the same location as the team leader, who is located at the headquarters and who is located near the key customer or other stakeholder.

Imbalanced Team: This configuration has a majority of team members in one location and minority groupings in all the other places. The majority group seem to dominate the decisions and have overpowering influence. The minority groups tend to feel an unequal status. They often become defensive and perhaps withdraw from the group or turn to other minority group members to try to gain some leverage. At a minimum, the imbalanced teams tend to share less information, are less cooperative and are more prone to conflict.

The majority group members often consider the minority team members as obstacles to progress and often ignore their situation-specific requirements, such as scheduling meetings at inconvenient hours or forgetting to include them in the decision-making process.

Team members on majority/minority configurations can have widely different experiences in the team. The majority group may believe that the team is functioning effectively, that the project is progressing well and that the right decisions are being made within the team. The minority team members, on the other hand, frequently feel ignored and inconvenienced, and issues that they consider to be highly relevant are not part of the group discussion. In general, majority/minority configurations result in more conflict than the balanced or 100% remote configurations.

In this section, I have explained why the Taco Sauce Test has increasing intensity depending on the type of configuration. However, these challenges are surmountable. Once the team analyze their configuration and understand the implications, they can actively strengthen the connections between the locations. There are many high performing virtual teams who ensure everyone feels included, create the closeness between remote team members and share information for creative ideas.

Case Study

Imagine a virtual team who are responsible for delivering a solution to a European client. The team consists of two account managers in France, three developers in India and four account managers in Spain. Manuel, the team leader, is also in Spain. Everyone is excited about the new customer and wants the project to succeed; however, the team does not function well together. Late replies on email are misinterpreted as a lack of commitment, and regular online meetings are dull as the agenda is filled with task updates and little discussion.

Any debates are dominated by the Spanish majority, as they seem to have a united front against the others.

The French have the perception that the decisions are predetermined and that their voices are not heard. Customer complaints and tight deadlines create tension in the team, revealing the country loyalties over team loyalty. The team members use cultural stereotypes to explain the behavior of colleagues in the other locations.

Manuel finds himself at the center of the disgruntled Spanish team, who easily walk down the hall to his office to complain about the failing project. He needs to be sympathetic to them, but he knows that he also needs the support of the team who are working in other locations in order to successfully deliver to the client. Manuel realizes that the team do not share information, do no listen to the ideas of their remote colleagues and do not work together toward shared goals.

This team has many issues, but the starting point for the diagnosis is the configuration. By looking at the team locations, we can uncover some of the sources of tension.

1. Hybrid Configuration: The team has a 5-3-2 configuration and the sub-groupings have formed based on location and culture. The team members across the locations do not know each other well, and instead of viewing their colleagues as unique individuals, categorize them into cultural subgroups. Also, they favor their local colleagues instead of supporting all team members. (See Chapter Three, Between the Locations.)

2. Majority/Minority Subgroupings: The majority Spaniards dominate with their opinions, and the French and Indian colleagues feel marginalized. Manuel is not facilitating discussions that include everyone's point of view and is yielding to the majority.

3. Team Leader Location: The local Spaniards have a disproportionate influence on the team leader which, the Indian and French team members notice and resent. Any perceived favoritism by the team leader is used as further ammunition for justifying low levels of collaboration.

From this simple and very common example, we immediately see the different layers of issues that negatively affect the team dynamic and therefore the outcome of the project. But herein lies the challenge: Most virtual teams have a configuration based on a strategic or practical need. So how can virtual teams build bridges across locations to create a highly functional and successful team that optimizes the use of global talent without succumbing to the potential pitfalls of global virtual teamwork?

Configuration is the Context
This question is answered throughout this book. This chapter reveals the context of virtual teams so that the other parts of the CALDO model and the solutions make sense. These solutions would include:

- Creating a shared team identity that supersedes local identities and inspires the team. This shared team identity counteracts the energy that separates team members with a spirit that connects them together.
- Recognizing, understanding and leveraging the cultural dynamics within the team so that everyone feels included and differences become a team advantage.
- Building relationships across locations so that the unique characteristics of each person override the cultural stereotypes.
- Organizing work for cross-location collaboration so the team members build trust and learn about each other's knowledge and competences.

- Engaging team members in the minority locations with procedures and activities that are inclusive and build bridges.

A Clever Solution

Diego is an IT Director of a global manufacturer with more than 25,000 people in locations all over the world. He has lived and worked in many countries and learned early in his career how cultural subgroupings can impact teams. When the company began a reorganization that accompanied a strategic shift from local to global, he and his colleagues created a new structure for the IT department. As Diego explained, "From the beginning we said that every team has to be 100% virtual. We saw that when there were many team members at one location and fewer at others, then the minorities suffered. The collaboration technology is improving, and if everyone is remote, then they are all in the same situation and have a better chance for teamwork." Even within a multinational organization with offices around the world, the department recognized the impact of configuration and created a 100% virtual organization, and the structure was a success.

It seems almost counterintuitive to deliberately construct 100% global virtual teams, and many people in Diego's department responded with disbelief when the policy was first announced. Sylvie in Singapore reflected on the team formation, "At first it was strange to work with someone I did not know. All I had was an email address. Most of us were surprised, since we had colleagues in the same building. But now many of us prefer it. We know each other well, and have built a remote team spirit. My remote colleagues think about issues differently, which makes the work interesting."

This example shows how leaders analyze the configuration of the virtual team, the context in the CALDO model, and can make changes that help collaboration. In this case, they specified the configuration. In other cases, team leaders accept the configuration and invest to create a well-connected, collaborative virtual team.

Co-located Blindness[2] Team members generally have a preference for the opinions and actions of their co-located colleagues, especially when virtual team members do not know each other well. A team member may hesitate to contact his remote colleague for a few reasons. For instance, he does not want to risk cultural miscommunication, he does not know how his colleague will react to the request for help and he does not know if his colleague is willing to apply her knowledge to his situation. On the other side, the remote colleague is glad not to be asked because she does not know how her expertise will be used by her remote colleague. When colleagues know each other, trust each other and have a shared goal that unites them together, these issues disappear.

Key Points

- The CALDO model is a holistic approach to a virtual team and considers how different elements of a team ultimately impact performance.
- The team configuration, meaning the location of the team members, is part of **context** of the CALDO Model because it can impact the quality of the teamwork across the locations.
- The hybrid virtual team, which is often the most common configuration in multinational organizations, is one of the most challenging configurations because of the formation of local subgroups.
- Team leaders and members can actively create a high performing

team in spite of the challenges of the configuration. For instance, by building the relationships and organizing shared tasks across the locations.

- Teams with isolate team members can benefit if the team member is a critical contributor or the team leader.

CHAPTER 2

Introduction to Cultural Diversity

Arend van Dijk and I worked together on an international project during the time of Y2K,[1] at the turn of the last century. That was the last time we saw each other, so when a mutual acquaintance recommended that I interview him for this book, I was glad to have a chance to reconnect with my past. Arend had gained broad global experience during the two decades in between. He was now head of IT projects for a logistics service provider and working across borders on a daily basis.

Arend's IT department is project based. "When a new client comes in, we form a project team consisting of the local contact in the country of the client for the language and customs, and the IT specialists on service applications, who are in different locations. For instance, the freight management specialists are in the US and the warehouse specialists are in the UK. This means that we always form an international project team who will be working virtually."

The IT specialists are in different locations due to the expansion history of the company. "Our company originated from Australia," explained Arend, "and grew through acquisitions of smaller suppliers who had their own IT specialists. With some of the larger acquisitions, we kept the people and expertise located where they were, and we added more resources and ultimately created centers of excellence. Now we tap into those colleagues depending on the need of the project."

This means that Arend and his colleagues are always working with people from other countries and cultures. "Even though we are a company that has been working like this for years, cultural differences still can have an impact," he continued.

Arend expanded on this topic and precisely described a situation that I encounter regularly, and what led me to write this book and develop the CALDO model.

"For instance," explained Arend, "recently we acquired a new IT location in India. Including them in our team has been a challenge for some of the guys. And I noticed that some of the team are more easily irritated than others. Some people are more curious, some are very closed. When we have issues, I try to coach the ones who struggle, but they read an email, or have a meeting and overreact because they don't see the other's point of view. In a web meeting, we see that the women in India are quiet, the ones in Spain are loud and the Americans are the first to speak. It doesn't matter if we are in the same room or if we are communicating virtually, we see the differences."

As Arend found with his teams, cultural differences between colleagues are evident when working virtually. I wanted to understand what happens when colleagues work across cultures virtually and bring their local ways of working to the virtual collaboration?

Take Your Culture to Work

When companies first began to work internationally, they often sent someone from headquarters to the new subsidiary to transfer knowledge and support the local company. These expats learned how to work in the new culture and often rose the career ladder as an experienced international executive. In the last two decades of the 1900s, reduced prices for air travel and a spike in the number of available flights corresponded with an increase in businesspeople who traveled for meetings, plant visits or to their place of work. It was not uncommon to travel to another city to work from Monday through Friday every week without the need to uproot the family. Cultural differences started registering as a legitimate topic of operational business. Managers were experiencing the frustrations, misunderstandings and delays caused by different ways of working between cultures. The cultural training and consulting industry grew as a result and a plethora of experts researched and wrote books about intercultural team dynamics, cultural sensitivity and mastering the art of working globally.

One of the first of these books about cultural diversity was *Riding the Waves of Culture* by Fons Trompenaars and Charles Hampden-Turner. Although the book had been assigned during an MBA course, it wasn't until I was dating my Dutch boyfriend (now husband) that I took the book off the shelf to look for answers to the question 'Why is he so different than my American boyfriends?' Fortunately, I found the answer in one of the dimensions, part of the Seven Dimension model that Trompenaars developed in the book. Seeing that dimension[2] was enough to help me understand my boyfriend and we have been enjoying multicultural marital harmony ever since.

The work of Trompenaars and Hampden-Turner was relevant for the business community because they could show how people from different countries commonly react when faced with the same dilemma. They summarized the outcome of the survey data into seven dimensions, which became a framework to explore cultural differences. The Seven Dimensions of Culture model is a guide for teams, colleagues and others to discuss cultural preferences and to delve deeper into understanding how cultural values influence others and ourselves.

Trompenaars was not the first, nor the last, to explain culture by using dimensions. Many college students have heard of Geert Hofstede, author of *Culture and Organizations: Software for the Mind*, assigned reading in courses as diverse as anthropology and international relations. And more recently, Erin Meyer provided more nuance to some of the cultural differences in her book *The Culture Map*. Many other consultants have also contributed their ideas on culture and intercultural teamwork, and this business-focused literature has helped people in organizations to increase their cultural intelligence, improve their cultural sensitivity and develop cultural agility.

All of these studies and resources are based on the assumption that multicultural colleagues meet each other regularly, and can sit together, share a meal and observe each other's behavior. Culture is visible, touchable and audible. Why does the director sit there? How close can I stand? Should I speak now or should I be quiet? And most importantly, when is lunch?

But what happens if we do not travel, sit together and have a common flip chart in front of us? Does culture still play a role?

As we examine virtual working, I would like to draw attention to the topic of cultural diversity. Cultural differences are alive and kicking in the global virtual team. This is the strength and challenge of the virtual teams, and the following chapters explore what this means.

What Is Culture?

What would you be like if you were born and raised in another country on another continent? How would you think and act? Do you think your habits and hobbies would be the same? Would you have selected the same type of life partner?

I often wonder how much of me is me, and how much has been molded because I was born and raised in the US, thus influenced by the culture of the US. This thinking highlights one of the characteristics of culture, that it is a social construct. People are not born with a culture but *into* a culture. It is through the socialization process that we learn and become attuned to the culture where we are. For instance, through our families, schools, friends, work and government system, we integrate the norms and values of our cultures into our own ways of being. Culture is relational and is passed on through human contact.

Most people find it easier to describe someone else's culture than their own. Why? Because it is hard to describe something that is normal and is much easier to describe the abnormal, the way many of us perceive the other cultures. Before trying to describe specific cultures, it helps to have a general understanding of what culture is.

To define culture, I will reference the work of Fons Trompenaars in his book *Riding the Waves of Culture.*[3] As Trompenaars explained by referencing anthropologist Clifford Geertz,

> "... *culture is the means by which people 'communicate, perpetuate, and develop their knowledge about attitudes towards life. Culture is the fabric of meaning in terms of which human beings interpret their experience and guide their action.... Cultures can be distinguished from each other by the differences in shared meanings they expect and attribute to their environment*'".

To highlight the various distinctions of culture, I prefer Trompenaars' explanation that culture is multilayered and how he modified a corporate culture model developed by Edward Schein for country culture (Figure 2.1).

The artifacts and behaviors are the things that we see, feel and hear when we are in a country. They are the symbols of a culture such as the architecture, language, food, sounds, clothes and other visible habits. These are often the first things travelers experience when they enter a new country.

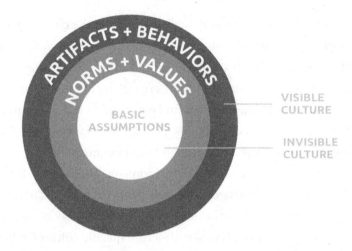

Figure 2.1 Layers of Culture

Trompenaars explains the next level of culture, "Norms are the mutual sense a group has of what is 'right' and 'wrong.' Norms can develop on a formal level as written laws, and on an informal level as social control. Values, on the other hand, determine the definition of 'good and bad', and are therefore closely related to the ideas shared by a group." For instance, a norm may be to show respect for older persons in a group or society. The value may be honor, loyalty or care, which are aspirational behaviors.

Finally basic assumptions is the level of culture we hardly discuss. This is the deep, implicit level of culture that gives energy to the norms and values and is expressed in the artifacts and behaviors. These are the assumptions about human relationships and human activity. How does a group of people make sense of the world in which they live together?

Culture Shock

When I lived in the US, we did not discuss the assumptions behind acceptable behaviors that drove our society. We were just being Americans. It wasn't until I worked in another culture that I was confronted by someone who had different basic assumptions, norms and values, and ultimately behaviors that caused me to experience culture shock, the moment of confusion resulting from the unexpected. It was at that moment, when my emotions oscillated from anger to frustration to confusion to withdrawal, that I realized we had a different way of being in the world, which translated to different work styles.

If you work internationally, you have probably experienced culture shock at some moment. The feeling of surprise, frustration, anger or uncertainty that arises when your colleagues work in a way that is different from your expectations. The feeling is normal. The impact of the culture shock on the collaboration is dependent on your response. Do you react from the anger and frustration, or do you reflect and respond with a behavior that tries to strive for deeper understanding, build collaborative bridges and leverage the diversity of thought?

Cultural Identity

For many of us, culture also defines our identity. We easily say 'I am Russian, Spanish, Chinese', or the culture to which we feel we belong. In general, the identity stays dormant until something activates the need for it to be expressed.[4] For instance, you may be Italian, living in Italy and working in a company with Italians. You will not feel the need to say 'I am Italian' because everyone else around you is also Italian. It is not until you work with someone who is not Italian that you begin to identify as Italian because you have an identity contrast. This is not a problem per se, unless it is activated due to conflict. These moments of activation, though, are also a time for reflection on your own identity and what that means for you. This always returns me to the question 'What would I be like if I were born and raised in another culture?' That question reminds me of the humanity we all share and that binds us together.

This book does not try to redefine culture, but builds on the work of others and asks the question 'What happens when we work virtually across cultures?' How do the norms, values and basic assumptions express themselves when people are collaborating and sitting in different countries?

The Pleasure and Pain of Cultural Diversity

"Before attending this workshop, I only thought of culture as a problem and I wanted to learn how to deal with the different cultures on my team. Now I realize it is also an opportunity where I need to put my attention."

These were the closing words of Stefano, a global project manager who attended one of my courses on cultural diversity and working virtually. Stefano's sentiment is not uncommon. Culturally diverse teams may struggle or flourish. The outcome is often dependent on how the team members engage with the cultural diversity in the team.

Many people find it challenging to work with colleagues from other cultures. They often find that communication takes more time and can result in misunderstandings. There is an unpredictability to the way colleagues might react to different situations. Most team members feel they need to step out of their comfort zone, which can add a layer of stress, particularly when timelines are tight. It is easier to work with colleagues who speak the same language, have the same expectations and share the same working habits.

On the other hand, culturally diverse teams have a creative potential that may be lacking in culturally homogeneous teams. Colleagues bring together their different backgrounds, working methods and experiences, and this can lead to innovation and ingenuity that only results from this cultural dynamic. Furthermore, the game-changing advantage of a culturally diverse virtual team is access to information about local markets. They understand the nuances and the local market context, and

24

can thereby strengthen the collective knowledge of the team. They have an expanded network of local stakeholders and local connections, which further enhances the team's knowledge base and potential reach.

Interestingly, the research on the impact of cultural diversity on virtual teams is mixed. Sometimes, the researchers find the benefits to be overwhelmingly positive and other times researchers describe only obstacles for collaboration.

Destroyers, Equalizers and Creators

Professors Joseph DiStefano and Martha Maznevski wrote an oft-cited article that shed light on the varying impacts of cultural diversity on global teams.[5] At the time of writing the article, they were at the International Institute for Management Development (IMD) and the University of Virginia, respectively. Through their research and consulting practice, they grouped global virtual teams into three performance categories:

Destroyers: These teams destroy value, waste time and lose energy. Team members do not trust each other, and they withhold information and use negative cultural stereotypes to justify their lack of collaboration. The potential of this team is far from being realized.

Equalizers: Team members think that the team is functioning well. Communication is good and the majority of the team attend meetings willingly and share information freely. The team complete the work and conflicts are avoided or resolved quickly. Yet the team are not realizing their full potential.

Leaders look at the teams and think 'so much talent, so much potential and yet… just ok.' The authors labeled these teams "Equalizers" because they seem to try to eliminate any cultural differences to make everything equal and easy. They wrote, "In a word - mediocrity."

Creators: Everyone wants to be on this team. They are high performance and exceed their expectations. Instead of minimizing cultural diversity, they exploit it by actively engaging in practices that are deliberately inclusive. Team members are encouraged to, and they want to, contribute their ideas, all of which leads to better and more creative solutions. Team members feel valued, respected and challenged.

The Creator teams leverage the diversity in the team and demonstrate the superior potential of global virtual teamwork.

I have worked with and coached teams that would fall into all of these three categories. Clearly, the Destroyer teams need to change, and external facilitation and team development programs may help. Often the team members start with good intentions, but events or attitudes take the team on a dangerous path.

I want to put a magnifying glass on the Equalizer category to understand what is happening. An example from my practice is when I worked with a hybrid team that had three people in Denmark and four in India. They implemented all the advised techniques for establishing a team such as clear deliverables, a team rhythm of meetings and an agreement on which communication tools to use for which task. But they never explored the cultural diversity on the team. They hoped the processes in place would result in a pleasant and effective working environment and avoid any conflict.

They also organized the tasks to avoid conflict. This meant that they preferred to assign tasks based on location, instead of across location, so that people from Denmark and India would work together.

Often when people join teams, they look for things that they have in common with their colleagues. Equalizer teams encourage conformity so that conversations flow and work is completed in the most conflict-free manner. The underlying assumption is that a discussion about cultural diversity would open a negative floodgate of conflict.

The reality is that the cultural differences exist. When I interviewed the team members, they mentioned annoyances and communication frustrations, but believed that was inherent in working internationally. They attributed any issues to the other location and did not see any forum to discuss and resolve.

Creator Teams

Creator teams acknowledge the cultural diversity on the team and explore what it means for their collaboration. They focus on the critical team processes when cultural diversity expresses itself and discuss the different ways of working beyond the stereotypes. For instance, they will investigate, sometimes with an external facilitator, how the team members approach communication, decision-making, giving feedback and other common business processes that can be culturally influenced.

When organizing tasks, Creator teams do not avoid cross-location sub-teams, acknowledging the benefits of cross-pollination of ideas when people work together. They invest the time and energy to understand the various perspectives on the team, recognizing that diverse views can lead to creative solutions if they are expressed in an inclusive environment.

They also value the role of a cultural bridge, a team member who has a connection with multiple cultures on the team and who can support the other team members to learn and integrate the cultures in the team.[6]

Underlying all of this, Creator teams support the development of cultural competence of each person on the team. They recognize this as a critical skill to work internationally, and regularly give each other feedback.

This book is for teams who want to become Creators. I often work with people who are in Equalizer teams. Although they may minimize cultural differences and try to keep everything steady, deep down they want to talk about culture because they know that it exists. They see the difference, they feel the difference, and yet it goes unspoken.

Equalizer teams can, however, break through their haze and become a high performance team. In the next section, I will show how cultural diversity plays a role in global virtual teams.

Key Points

- Although cultural diversity has been researched for years, cultural dynamics in the virtual context is a more recent topic.
- Virtual team members must develop cultural competence while working in their own location. Previously, people working internationally tended to travel or relocate and therefore were more immersed in other cultures.
- Multicultural virtual teams can be categorized into Destroyer, Equalizer or Creator. Creator teams acknowledge and incorporate the cultural diversity on the team.

Three Ways Culture Impacts Global Virtual Teams

People on global virtual teams have more reasons to develop cultural competence than people on multicultural co-located teams. This may seem paradoxical since virtual team members sit in their own countries and breath in the air of their own cultures. But they are still part of a multicultural team, and the underlying component of geographic distance can create the conditions for culture to be even more impactful. In this section, I will use theory and concrete examples to explain how culture impacts virtual teams. You will see why cultural diversity is a critical element at the center of the CALDO model.

This chapter has three sections based on how cultural diversity impacts global virtual teams.

I. Culture within the Team: This section expands on the work of thought leaders who have written about cultural diversity by looking at examples within virtual teams.

II. Culture between the Locations: Team members may think differently about their local colleagues compared to their distant colleagues. Culture is a common identifier to create subgroups.

III. Culture outside the Team: The team may be surprised as to how the cultural environments where the team members are located can have consequences for virtual team.

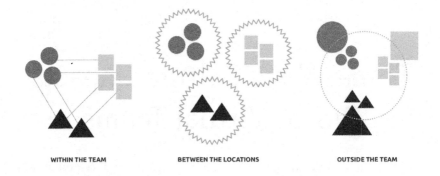

WITHIN THE TEAM   BETWEEN THE LOCATIONS   OUTSIDE THE TEAM

I. Within the Team

This book is 'standing on the shoulders of giants,' so to speak. It is built on the extensive and ground-breaking work of researchers, practitioners and writers of the past who have made contributions to the fields of anthropology, culture and business. Cultural diversity within the organizational context is a relatively new field in business study. Pioneers

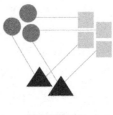

WITHIN THE TEAM

such as Geert Hofstede, Fons Trompenaars, Edward T. Hall and, more recently, Erin Meyer have researched and written to advance the understanding of the international and multicultural workplace.

I am building on their work by asking, "What happens when we work virtually?" The research shows that team members bring their cultural norms and assumptions to the virtual space as well, creating a multicultural environment.

This may seem counterintuitive, since the team member sits in her own country, eating her local foods and communicating with her local colleagues in her own language and style. But as soon as she attends an online meeting, participates in a chat or calls a remote colleague, she encounters cultural diversity, without ever leaving her country.

Culture impacts a virtual team in three ways, the first is between the team members. This section contains stories that you may recognize in your own experience. A message throughout this book is that successful virtual team members develop cultural competence. The first step is to recognize cultural diversity, even in the virtual team.

How Often to Follow Up?

I met Bill in one of my courses when he was the Director of Manufacturing for the Americas region of a global packaging company located in Chicago. The "Americas" meant North and South America in this company, and his team was located throughout the region. Even though Bill was a very experienced professional, he had an 'aha' moment when his colleague Gabriela from Mexico explained the culture of her country. Gabriela was answering the question as to whether the team leader needs to follow up with each person individually after the team finishes a meeting and agrees on the tasks. "Yes, absolutely," Gabriela began. "When a leader follows up with an employee a few things happen. First, you are showing that the work is important and a priority for the person. Afterall, they have many priorities, and especially when you are remote, you need to emphasize the task for the employee. Second, the contact itself is a chance to build the connection between each other, and to build the relationship. When you take an interest in the employee, you are showing that you care for him, and that helps with their motivation. The follow-up call or video meeting can have a powerful impact and is an important task for the team leader."

I saw the surprise on Bill's face, particularly when someone from Brazil contributed, "That is true for us as well." In the US, managers would not follow up after tasks were assigned and agreed during a meeting because that would be a sign of lack of trust. If a team member agrees to a task at a meeting, then everyone should assume he will do it. As Bill explained, "When we have our virtual team meetings, I ensure that the objectives and tasks are clear and everyone has agreed. I also emphasize that they can contact me if they have a problem. One of my team members in Mexico City has not been performing, and he doesn't reach out to me with problems. But I have not contacted and followed up with him, as I didn't want him to think that I don't trust him. I had not realized he was waiting for me!"

One person's annoying phone call is another person's opportunity to connect. For some cultures, the relationship is the starting point of working together. Through knowing each other, colleagues can build trust, understand each other's unique personal needs and play to each other's strengths. Other cultures, on the other hand, rely on the work itself as the basis for building connection. These colleagues commit to a task and try to complete it as a means of showing they are trustworthy.

The Environmental Impact

Another cultural consideration is how confident people are that the assumptions in a plan will be the reality when doing the work. In some cultures, there is an inherent belief that the environment is stable enough and that they have the agency to carry out the planned work. Other cultures, on the other hand, view the environment as continuously changing, and therefore, plans need to be regularly checked for the reality in which they operate.

Bill, and many other Americans, intrinsically believe that the conditions for the plan are stable, whereas the Mexican colleagues believe the environment can impact their plans in unpredictable ways. In Mexico, when the team leader calls the employee, they can update each other with the latest information and check that the plan is still possible.

After the course, Bill pledged to call his team members in South America more often. This is a start, and the Mexican colleagues also have an opportunity to develop new behaviors. Through building the relationships, Bill and the team can create a team environment in which the team members feel comfortable to reach out to Bill when they have a problem.

I'm Not Your Dear!

As I was born and raised in the US, I was taught a direct communication style. 'Get to the point,' 'start with the end in mind,' and 'don't waste time because time is money,' are all idioms that are intrinsically intertwined with American culture and way of thinking. Communication is therefore crisp, brief and efficient.

With this background, I felt a great deal of sympathy when I heard the story told by Julien, a gentle Swiss financial analyst who had received feedback on the way he wrote emails to his colleagues in Colombia.

"I was told that I never use the word 'dear' and that I don't ask how they are doing." We all started laughing because the way Julien told the story made it sound like it was the craziest thing he had ever encountered at work. Julien explained his situation in more detail.

"In the German part of Switzerland, we are efficient and business-like in our writing and the way we communicate. Adding 'dear' and 'how are you' is perceived as a waste of time. I work regularly with the shared service center in Panama and send emails all the time to different people with instructions and requests. My communication is quick and to the point. But they didn't like this. We were having a quarterly review of our cooperation and a woman mentioned it. I was really surprised!"

In some cultures such as Switzerland, work relationships are based on the work and the output. They call work relationships *professional* because they consider them to be different than a social relationship, which is outside of work. They focus on the task at hand and think of their colleagues as people associated with the work. They do not inquire too much about a person's private life because that may cross some boundaries, which would make them feel uncomfortable. I had made this mistake in Germany when I asked some people at lunch about their hobbies. In a matter-of-fact tone, the German responded, "We don't ask those types of questions here." I was about to cross the boundary into personal space and had been gently reminded to return to acceptable work topics.

Maria from Panama had a smile on her face and was warm and friendly from the first moment we saw each other on the video. We started the conversation by talking about our respective backgrounds and she smiled the whole time and showed genuine interest. I felt at ease with her. We were discussing a potential course and I took the opportunity to ask her about communication with Switzerland.

"Sometimes the emails can come across as being really harsh," she said. "They are very direct, not friendly at all. Sometimes the Swiss don't even write our names, but just give an instruction with a due date. We in Panama are friendlier and like to take an interest in each other. It is our way of getting close to each other even though it is just email. It shows that we are people."

It may seem like an inefficient ritual in some cultures, but greetings to open and close communications can indicate a willingness to be open with and respectful toward a colleague. Some cultures do not want to work with just productive people but with colleagues whom they like and enjoy. This focus on the relationship can also impact trust and a willingness to help, particularly when someone is in a difficult situation.

In the end, Julien started to use friendlier greetings in his communication with his colleagues. He shrugged his shoulders when he said, "I got used to it. Actually, I went beyond just the emails and tried to be friendlier in the videos and conference calls as well. It really did seem to improve the working relationship."

This story is not about emails per se, but about communication and relationships across the geographies. When people work across cultures, they have the opportunity to learn new behaviors that may not have made sense in their local culture, but are appropriate in the global context. Through the cross-cultural collaboration, both Julien and Maria were confronted with another style of communication, different from their own. To develop cultural competence, both of them can examine their cultural norms and experiment with new behaviors with their virtual colleagues.

When Loud Is Too Loud, Quiet Too Quiet

"And people from Asia are always quiet, they just don't speak up during the calls," vented Boris, an HR partner in Moscow who was explaining the issues with working virtually between Europe and Asia. Emika and Sherry were also on the call from Singapore. Emika did not verbally disagree with this statement, but clearly proved it wrong by being very vocal during the call and by having a strong influence on the direction we were taking with the work.

So much for stereotypes! But was Boris so wrong? He is not the first global manager to express this observation. Whenever I hear the words 'the Chinese are quiet and never speak up,' I have a flashback to a course I gave many years ago, early in my career.

The course was part of a high potential program and the days were long and intense. The participants were new hires of a global shipping giant and had just started a two-year management development program in which they would be located in another part of the world every six months. For this reason, understanding culture was part of the curriculum and was well received.

The participants were young, energetic and engaged. Whenever I offered a case, people quickly raised their hands to give their opinions. They had fun exploring the topic in the groups and I could see that they were learning from each other.

During one of the breaks, Kelly, a Chinese woman, approached me. She asked about my background, and I asked about her experience in the program. It was a very nice conversation. Before she left me to get a drink, she said, "Call on the Chinese students sometimes," before she smiling and turning away.

And she was right. Although there were many people speaking up and offering opinions, very few were from China, and this was one of the countries with the largest representation of participants. As an American trainer, I engage with participants who take an active role during training seminars. In fact, calling on someone who has not raised their hand could put them on the spot or embarrass them in front of everyone. It might even be considered unkind or inappropriate. The hand raising is a signal from the participant to the trainer that there is a willingness to talk in the group.

If the Chinese participants were not going to raise their hands, and yet wanted to participate, how would I know? I quickly needed a new strategy. Kelly was not speaking only for herself, but for a group of people who were feeling left out. I needed to consider another signal and decided to look more at people's faces. From that moment, I called on people with their hands in the air or with the look of readiness on their face as a signal of a willingness to share their opinion. At first, I was uncomfortable and uncertain if I would misjudge a facial expression, so I called on Kelly first. She gave her opinion, with a knowing smile that I had listened to her. From there I felt more comfortable calling on others only by looking at their faces.

Chinese students learn very early in school that they only give their opinion when the teacher calls on them. A common Confucius saying is: "A superior man is modest in his speech but exceeds in his actions." Colleagues from Asia will tend to wait for others to speak first as a sign of respect and as a way to ensure that what they say will make sense. They also have a strong aversion to being wrong so that they do not lose face.

Colleagues from other cultures may have varying degrees of willingness to share their opinion in a meeting. The Swedes may take their time to respond and to speak in a tone that is considered emotionless by the Italians, but overly passionate by the Finns. Colleagues from India will tend to be reserved, especially if someone more senior is on the call.

A leader of an inclusive global virtual team will provide the time for people to contribute their opinions and then sense the right moment to ask the others who have not yet spoken for their opinions on a matter. In this way, all voices can be heard with respect.

What Do Words Mean?

Japan poses an interesting paradox for the study of intercultural global business. On the one hand, the economic strength of the country means that it has powerful influence in the world and has become an attractive location for multinationals. On the other hand, the island nature of the country and the historically closed culture means that Japanese society has not been greatly influenced by other cultures. It can therefore be a bit of a puzzle for global virtual teams working with Japanese colleagues. I was glad to have an interview with Akinari, Head of Engineering Projects in Japan. Akinari has lived in the US and Sweden and was able to articulate the unique characteristics of the Japanese culture, particularly in the context of global teams.

Similar to Erin Meyer's chapter on communicating ("Listening to the

Air"),[1] Akinari explained how the Japanese use words and body language to communicate. "Much of Japanese communication is non-verbal," Akinari explained during our first video call. "We communicate with five senses, and sometimes with six senses. It is difficult to say, but we take in the atmosphere of the place of meeting to understand each other. Not the verbal. We are working in the same narrow space together for a long time, not only the day, but years, 10-15 years. We know each other very well. Day by day accumulation of knowledge about each other builds up so that we can sense what the other people think with less verbal communication. Maybe it is because we are a single ethnicity living on an isolated island country," he provided as way of explanation for this unique ability to communicate.

Akinari continued to share his observations. "For example, a manager like me doesn't need to give directions verbally. I do not need to say everything to the subordinate what they need to do. They could feel and understand what I want to have. The subordinate somehow can understand what the manager is thinking because we have been working so long together."

Anthropologist Edward T. Hall distinguished two different types of communication patterns in his book *Beyond Culture*[2] "High context" communication means that the spoken words are infused with more meaning than just the words themselves. People in high-context cultures understand what is being communicated not just by the words but also because they understand the context in which the words are spoken, they know the person who is speaking very well and they look for clues between the words to understand the entire message.

An example is when people say 'yes' when they mean 'no.' Colleagues from the same culture will understand the meaning of 'no' by the tone of the voice, and by the words that are used. "It's as if I said 'no,'" explained my Brazilian friend Marcia, "but to say 'no' would come across as rude, and that would make everyone uncomfortable."

In the Netherlands, by contrast, to say what you really think is a sign of respect. If you don't like an idea or want to say 'no,' then say it. The Netherlands is a country of "low context" communication, meaning that one does not have to know the context or the person well to understand the meaning of the message. The spoken words deliver the full meaning.

Johan, our Dutch friend, chimed in during a lunch with Marcia and me, "We don't like when people are indirect. It comes across as sneaky and dishonest and quite frankly disrespectful. In our minds we think 'why didn't he just tell me that he could not do it?'"

The Dutch pride themselves on being open, transparent and direct. Unfortunately, this directness is often interpreted as rudeness. The Dutch are being respectful by using words that directly convey the exact message.

Communication Context and Global Virtual Teams

Throughout the course of this book, I often mention the role that technology plays in both facilitating and undermining global virtual teams. Technology, as it relates to communication, also influences the context of communication and therefore can have an inadvertent result on the message being delivered.

For example, by design, email is made for direct, low-context communication. Hence, it will be wholly inadequate as a communication tool for colleagues from high context cultures. They would prefer richer communication tools that convey symbols and cues that provide more meaning, such as video or phone.

I consulted for a CEO from a Mexican company who wanted his direct reports in Germany to always have a video meeting. The Germans complained because at the time video was difficult to schedule. It required space in a private room, whereas the phone was always available. For the Mexican leader, however, hearing only the voices of his team was not sufficient. He wanted to see his colleagues so that he could read their facial expressions and see their eyes. He needed these communication cues to give more meaning to the contextual communication.

Communication's Starting Point

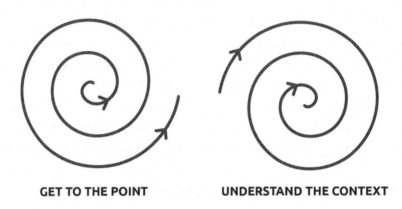

GET TO THE POINT **UNDERSTAND THE CONTEXT**

Figure 3.1 Types of Communication Flow

Understanding communication deepens further when we consider how global teams use language and explain their points of view. Erin Meyer called this the art of persuasion and recognized that it can have an impact on how the meeting is organized and how topics are discussed.[3]

Meyer explained that some cultures had a "principles first" reasoning in which they begin with the big picture and then draw the conclusion. They want to understand the entire context, the history of the project and all the stakeholders that will be impacted. Armed with that information and reasoning, they can make a decision on the specific issue of the team.

"Applications first" reasoning, by contrast, means to look at the details of the issue and use that as a basis to get started. In "applications first" cultures, they want to get to the point, think about the issues at hand and consider the principles later. They tend to think in bullet points.

As is encouraged in America, I am very much an "applications first" type, but I have learned to appreciate the reasoning of my "principles first" colleagues, starting with my Turkish colleague Feza. She always started her explanations with 'It's like this' and would explain the situation with metaphors, historical characters and an emphasis on critical links. Through listening to Feza, I began to appreciate the complexities of situations more and the subtle opportunities that I may have missed in my race to the details. I also applied that style in conversations with colleagues from Poland, China, Italy and many other countries.

The ideal global virtual team includes both types of communication styles. Teams with members who remind the team to think about the big picture and other members who get the team to focus on what needs to be done are better able to handle complex problems with creative solutions. As Fons Trompenaars often mentions, the ability to recognize, respect and reconcile the differences of diversity makes the team stronger.

Specific and Diffuse

Global managers who are hiring talent for a position in the US will receive a resume with the candidate's education, work history, achievements and career goals. With this information, the hiring manager determines whether the candidate has the right skills and competence for the job and will then invite the person for an interview. During the interview, they will discuss her career, training and experience in order to gain a better understanding of whether she can do the job.

This was explained very clearly by my friend and colleague Tucker Miller, attorney, to a room full of German managers and directors who recruited and worked with colleagues in the US. The multinational company hired Tucker and me to explain the legal and cultural environment in the US.

"But how can we judge if a person is the right fit on so little information?"

asked a German director, clearly perplexed by what he perceived as restrictive. "I need to know the whole person," he continued, "his or her age, marital status, family life and a photo should all be on the CV. And I should be able to discuss this during the interview. How will I ever know if that person can work with us?"

"You will know they can work with you by judging them based on their work," Tucker replied. "Most good recruiting agencies will remove the picture and delete age-related information before giving the resumes to you. In the US, managers should not be using this personal information to judge the professional qualities of a candidate. This is what gets people in legal trouble," Tucker explained.

The German managers were silent. They realized they would have to change their ways of working in the US. Essentially, they would be recruiting new talent based on what they considered only partial information.

In the Seven Dimensions Model of Culture, Fons Trompenaars identified a dimension called Specific vs. Diffuse.[4] It is a very rich dimension covering many aspects of cultural diversity, including the nuance of whether people consider the whole (Diffuse) or the parts (Specific).

Virtual teams experience an expression of this dimension in how team members approach their work and personal lives. The Specific culture team members speak about work, focus on the task at hand, share information and get down to work. They often have a strict delineation between work relationships and private relationships, and typically they are very protective of their private time. When the workday is done, they turn off their computer and join their families and friends for social activities.

Diffuse cultures have a contrasting view. They have a more holistic approach to work relationships. Keeping their private lives separate from their professional lives is setting up an artificial barrier. They consider their colleagues to be as close as friends.

Why Be Close?

A few years ago, I facilitated a team event to explore the cultural diversity within the virtual management team of a relatively new joint venture. The timing was perfect because the team had worked together long enough to already have issues to discuss, but still early enough to think kindly about each other. The joint venture comprised a Dutch and a French headquarters and so the participants were either Dutch or French, based on the company locations.

As part of the preparation, I interviewed everyone and concluded that the cultural groupings had different expectations on how to work together. I designed the workshop to explore culture in their own situation. As we discussed the Specific vs Diffuse dimension as expressed in their team, Pierre, a reflective Frenchman, offered a thoughtful insight into his own culture.

"When we speak about building relationships," he began, "it is not because we like drinking good wine or eating lunch together. We are spending time together to learn about each other. I want to know how my colleagues think, what is important to them, how they react, what distracts them or makes them angry. Then I can work with them in a way that uses their abilities, avoids their irritations, let's them know that I care for them and am someone they can trust. Without this information, I am just sending emails to a stranger," Pierre concluded.

Virtual team members from Specific cultures may find a few minutes before the video meeting to discuss the weather is enough interaction to establish a friendly working relationship. They do not need to know more about the person in order to work together effectively.

For virtual team members from Diffuse cultures, the pre-meeting weather report may not be enough to make them feel comfortable. They prefer meetings that are not only work-focused but also people-focused. They are interested in their colleagues and struggle to work with them if they do not know them well. They are willing to invest the time because through the relationship they can collaborate better together.

By the nature of virtual teams, colleagues have geographic distance between each other. As they collaborate, different team members may try to bridge the distance and build the relationship in different ways, which may be influenced by their cultural values.

Up and Down the Hierarchy

Sven described how teams work together in Sweden. Everyone contributes their point of view, and through discussion and consensus they make a decision together. Sven and his Swedish colleagues admitted that the process is time-consuming, but they feel this is the best way to operate as a virtual team as well.

"Well, then don't include an Italian," countered Giandomenico, "because you will put them in a very awkward situation and cause them a lot of stress. They would feel pressure from you to act as if everyone is equal, but knowing full well that they need to consult with and include their manager in the office. You would put them in a bind."

Organizational hierarchy is a topic that is covered in most existing cultural models such as those created by Erin Meyer (Egalitarian-Hierarchical),[5] Fons Trompenaars (Achievement-Ascription)[6] and Geert Hofstede (Power Distance).[7] In some cultures, leaders have a prominent role in directing and guiding the organization, while in other organizations they have a more hands-off role of coaching and strategy.

Jia-Xin in Singapore was responsible for a regional team and was surprised by how the hierarchy played out in the project dynamic. The team consisted of people from three countries: two from Australia, three from India and two from Singapore. Jai-Xin is highly educated and grew up in Singapore, a country rich in diversity of cultures living together. Singapore plays an important role in being the bridge between the East and West, and people who live in the cosmopolitan city-state are continuously bumping into expats, visitors and people from other cultures. Still, Jia-Xin was shocked.

"I was promoted as the head of the IT development team and was excited about the position," she said enthusiastically. One of her first projects was to integrate the IT department of a new acquisition in Australia with the IT Shared Services Center in India. The Australian company had IT applications, which were new to the group, so they wanted to bring them into the standard process.

"What was surprising to me," Jia-Xin explained, "was how uninterested the management of Australia was in our project. I would call them to confirm some of the decisions and their answers were something like, 'Why are you bothering me? Talk to the Australians on the team, they can handle these issues.' In my view, keeping the team leader informed is required and it is a way to ensure that our decisions are aligned with what they want. I thought I was doing the right thing, speaking from manager to manager, and although they were polite, they were not interested. I felt this was risky for the project, that the decisions of the team members might not be checked and aligned with the location directors."

Brian, in Australia, whom the manager Jia-Xin contacted, had a different perspective. "I am definitely interested in the project and want it to succeed. It is part of our integration strategy and I discussed it with Dirk and Robert when they first started. Although I touch base with them to talk high level, I do not need to go into the details of every decision. They can handle that. Actually, every time Jia-Xin calls me to discuss the project, the two guys feel undermined. It really doesn't help their confidence, especially with the uncertainty that comes with acquisitions. They want to make a good impression," Brian said, demonstrating sympathy with his Australian colleagues.

Whatever the leader's style, some people on the team will prefer it and some others will expect something completely different. Through conversations and practice, the team will develop norms. But since many global teams are part of a matrix organization, team members may feel the pressure between the team and their other managers, as Giandomenico mentioned earlier. An effective and caring global team leader will recognize the tension and develop solutions that work for the team and other key stakeholders.

II. Between the Locations

As mentioned in the section titled Team Configuration, hybrid virtual teams are the most challenging configuration because of the potential formation of subgroups by location, and often by culture. This is the second way that cultural diversity impacts multicultural virtual teams. I titled this section *between the locations* because cultural stereotypes become one of the expressions of the subgroup formation.

BETWEEN THE LOCATIONS

Although they are challenging, hybrid virtual teams have the potential to achieve results beyond a co-located team. Team members can be located where the 'action' is, be that a strategic client, an integrated supplier or other key stakeholder. Having more than one person in that location can provide the critical mass to leverage the relationship or to keep abreast of new developments.

Another reason for hybrid teams may be the organizational structure. The talented people on the virtual team are located where the company assets are, for instance, in the factory, R&D labs or center of excellence.

Finally, by coincidence, more than one person on the team live and work in the same location. They are important for the team and are all necessary for the team's success.

Once the team leader and members understand why hybrid teams are challenging, they can take the actions to counter the subgroup tendency and realize the benefits of the hybrid virtual team.

When Distance Becomes Abstract

Think of a day in your agenda three months from now. Perhaps you have a few things blocked in your calendar, but it is fairly vague. You don't have all of the details on how the day will come together, with whom you will interact, how you will move through the day or deal with the weather. Most likely you do not feel an emotional connection with that day.

Now think of your agenda for tomorrow. You most likely know the details, how you will move through the day, whom you will see, how you will prepare, what you will wear, where you will be and when. You may even have an emotional reaction, such as dread a certain meeting, excited to see a former colleague or happy that the weather will be nice.

As humans, we view events that are nearby in detail and those that are far away as more abstract. We do this with people as well.

When we work with co-located and distant colleagues, we often experience this phenomenon, explained by Construal Level Theory.[8] We can give detailed descriptions of our colleagues nearby such as 'Sue was interactive in the last meeting,' 'Johan prefers to speak in the morning' and 'Saskia contributed great ideas yesterday.' But we usually use abstract descriptions for our remote colleagues, such as 'They are Russian.' We do not know the individuals well enough to distinguish them from each other. We tend to use more abstract, less nuanced words to describe them.

Professors Wilson, Crisp and Mortenson of William & Mary, Abilene Christian University and INSEAD, respectively, applied Construal Level

Theory to virtual teams as a means to understand the formation of subgroups.[9] They explained that physical distance can lead to psychological distance, which is how one feels about something in terms of close or far in relation to themselves. The psychological distance then leads to an abstract level of thinking about the person or object.

This can have a significant impact on how teams work together because it can be the basis for an 'us vs them' mentality and corresponding behaviors.

The Role of Culture in Psychological Distance

According to the professors, cultural differences can also contribute to a feeling of psychological distance. When people hear a language that is unusual and observe behaviors that are counter to expectations, they may feel less close to that person. This may be an initial reaction, and can be lessened through conversations, lunches together and deeper knowledge of each other. In a virtual team, however, the cultural differences combined with the physical distance can strengthen the psychological distance and the use of abstract thinking of the others.

To understand how the abstract thinking of remote colleagues forms 'us vs them' subgroups on virtual teams, I turned to a psychologist, Claudia Crisan. Claudia is a practicing Jungian Psychotherapist as well as a Learning & Development and Culture & Engagement Lead for Europe Functions and Categories for PepsiCo, located in Romania. With this background, she was the ideal expert to explain how the human mind and behaviors at work are connected. She began with the concept of duality as the basis to understand the impact of culture on a multi-location virtual team.

"Consciousness is formed through duality," she began. "You have to perceive the opposite in order to define some object. For instance, you can define a mountain only when you have a valley to contrast. When you see the object for itself, when you see its shape and its limits, what it is and what it is not, you can start to even further define more detailed things such as whether it is a rocky mountain or a tree-lined mountain."

When people work on a global virtual team, an easily accessible contrast is the culture between locations. Afterall, culture is associated with a region or country; it is sometimes heard in accents, and it is noticed when colleagues begin to work together. The duality is easily established and is the reason the cultural identity in each person is triggered. When people work co-located with people from the same culture, cultural identity and the need for cultural boundaries are dormant. However, many people begin to identify with their culture when they are in a group of contrasts.

Turning to the Local Colleague

Claudia continued, "Whenever we meet someone new, we have a need for socializing. It is an innate need we have, but also the need of protecting and preserving what is ours. This latter need is kept alive through defense mechanisms. Another way to put this is that we are constantly bouncing between the individual need, that of adaptation, which offers novelty and individual development, and the need to be loyal to the collective, which offers safety. I am different, and because I am different there is also potential for problems. This activates our instinctual need for preserving what has worked for us for such a long time in the past."

To avoid uncertainty and potential problems, we turn to that which is familiar. In the case of global virtual teams, the familiar is our local colleagues. We understand their language, their way of working, their references and their background. We can usually comprehend their point of view, and we have similar norms and ways of being. The connection is easy, seamless and effective. 'Them over there' becomes a reference for team members who are unpredictable, hard to understand and dare I use the word 'strange.'

'Us vs Them' Tripod

I can summarize the phenomenon in three points:

1. We think of remote colleagues as psychologically distant and in more abstract terms.
2. Subgroups by location often use culture as the level of abstraction to define the duality.
3. The predictability of the local colleagues contrasts with the unpredictability of the distant colleagues, thereby contributing to the subgroups distinction.

These three points create the legs of the 'us vs them' tripod.

This problem can have a profound impact on how a hybrid team collaborates. The people in the different locations refer to the other colleagues in abstract terms, and often use negative cultural stereotypes. You might hear phrases like "they are always late," "they never understand," and "they take forever to get to their point." And each location subgroup looks for behavior to confirm their stereotypical image.

Each team may experience this phenomenon differently. At a mild level of 'us vs them,' the team members favor the ideas of local colleagues. At an extreme level, the location subgroups blame each other, stop sharing information and stop listening to each other.

Learning about the Other

Despite the danger that subgroups pose to hybrid virtual teams, a negative impact is not inevitable. Returning to Claudia one more time, she explained, "The more knowledge you have about something, the more detail you can distinguish. Once you know and accept the mountain, you can learn about its trees, pathways, and rivers." In the same way, team members can learn about each other's cultures, their communication styles and their work ethics so that these stop being sources of differentiation and instead become sources of enrichment. They can then discover and appreciate the unique characteristics of each person, regardless of the location.

III. Outside the Team

When a co-located team ends a meeting, everyone leaves the meeting room into the same hallway. They work in the same building, probably eat a similar lunch in the canteen, have the same HR policies, are under the same tax regulations, deal with the same traffic, experience the same weather and encounter similar social pressures. They work within the same environment or system.

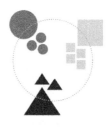

OUTSIDE THE TEAM

When a virtual team turn off the video and close their laptops, everyone looks out the window and sees something different. Each person deals with different traffic, eats in a different canteen, experiences different weather, has different HR policies, has different tax regulations, and faces different social pressures. The team members are working in different environments or local systems and cultures.

These local systems are the third way in which culture can impact a virtual team, often with unexpected consequences.

Teams form norms and ways of working either explicitly or implicitly. I recommend that multicultural teams discuss in the early stages of the team formation how they will work together and how they will engage with stakeholders. Virtual team members come with various assumptions and expectations, and this can cause conflict if not addressed early. The team will ultimately form their own unique culture that includes working methods and practices, which may be different from those of the local cultures.

The Virtual Team amongst the Local Cultures

Professors Catherine Durnell Cramton and Pamela J. Hinds of George Mason University and Stanford University, respectively, observed the interplay between the virtual team and the local organization in a longitudinal study of multiple teams composed of members from Germany, India and the US.[10] They found that team members and managers often had to resolve contradictions that arose as a result of the collaboration. I recognized many of their observations from my work as well.

The tensions within the team are often a surprise to the team leader, and resolving these tensions takes dedicated time and effort. New tensions are always around the corner. Successful team leaders have excellent listening skills, are curious and are culturally competent. This skill set perfectly described Goran, a leader of a multicultural virtual team.

I met Goran when he was a participant in one of my workshops, and I quickly realized that he had a reflective way of approaching his team. I interviewed Goran, as well as his manager and someone from his team. Since I spoke with Goran a few times over the course of a year, I was able to have a picture of the full story from different angles over time.

Goran and his manager Kevin had a challenge. They were managers of an insurance company with actuarial work at the headquarters in London and processing work in India. The team in London analyzed the request, and the team in India processed the data as per instructions from the London office. Emails for this setup provided sufficient communication between the two sites, and the manager of the India team was a focal point for any communication outside of normal processing. All went well until an increase in sales and stricter regulatory requirements increased the volume of work. The analysis team in London expanded by hiring expensive contractors, thereby exploding expenses much to the consternation of the director. He wanted to get costs under control. Goran and Kevin had to find a solution.

They decided to reconsider the work of the team members in India. As Goran explained, "It was very easy to underestimate what they could do. When we changed their role, they were able to contribute to the business in a different, value-adding way." But the new work process required more than a snap of the fingers.

Goran and Kevin had a vision. They wanted the Indian team to change from processing work to more complicated case analysis. They also wanted the interaction between the Mubai and London locations to be seamless, with questions and answers going directly between the applicable persons. This was a 180-degree change from the previous setup, and the new way of working had a heavy cultural influence from London.

To look at Goran's story, I would like to use a simplified version (Figure 3.2) of a model developed by Hinds and Durnell Cramton.

Team Practice: The norm within the team. Sometimes this will be in the team charter, or develop over time.

Tension: The conflict between a team norm and the local company to which one or more team members belong.

Resolution: How the team and local company together address the tension.

Team Practice: Goran provided more details. "To be able to do the actuarial work, the Indian team members would need to take on more responsibility, contact us when they had questions or doubts, and be proactive with problem solving. We needed them to work as we do in London, and we tried to implement this in the team right away.

"The first step was to ask them to contact us more frequently and to open the lines of communication, even from junior people. But this was completely new for Indian people. We are in HQ, after all, and this can

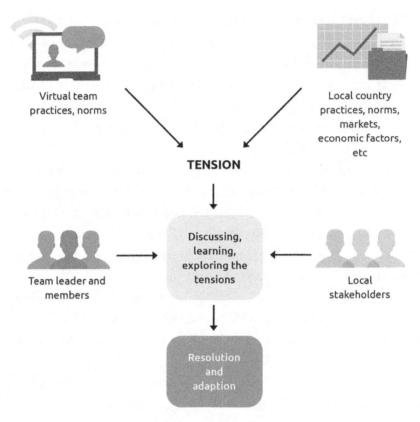

Figure 3.2 Impact of Culture from Outside of the Team

be intimidating. To make this change, we had weekly video calls with all team members so that they can see we are humans. I had 30 minute one-on-one calls with each person in India every two weeks during which we did not talk about work. I asked them about themselves, work-life balance, and studying for the actuarial exam. I was trying to make them feel comfortable with me so that they would reach out when they had an issue. The other London colleagues tried to open lines of communication as well. After one year, yes, one year, we were able to change their behavior and now they contact us regularly."

Tension: The Mumbai team emulated the working style of the London team, but not without tension within their local cultural system, and the Indian manager of the team in particular. He had been educated and promoted on the assumption that once he became a manager, he would be in charge of the team. With his position came certain responsibilities as well as boundaries, part of which meant that he would be the point of contact for the London team. The open communication between the London and Mumbai team members, however, actually complicated his work. How could he make decisions for the team if he did not know what was going on? Also, he was asked to be more flexible and responsive to the workflow that previously had always been a defined process. As the process leader he had control; however, the new way of working led to a loss of control. People were working more independently, and he did not have the overview of what everyone was doing.

Initial resolution: Goran tried to coach the Indian manager to become more like a London manager, with less emphasis on control and more focus on facilitation and strategy. "Afterall," explained Goran, "his team was receiving more responsibility, which would be good for him and his career."

In fact, the team was doing so well that they received the Team of the Year award for the entire Indian organization. Quite an honor! Although the Indian manager understood the change, and although he was receiving coaching from the London managers, he did not have a reference or example amongst his peers in India. He saw how they managed teams, which was aligned with his expectations of how he wanted to manage his team. He recognized that his team was the exception. When he went to lunch with his local manager colleagues, he did not have anyone as a sounding board to discuss his experience, his concerns or his challenges. Eventually the difference was too great a burden for him, and he left the company.

55

Resolution: To fill the leadership vacuum, Goran and Kevin promoted someone from the team. After all, she understood the new way of working and had already adapted to the London style.

A few months later, I interviewed Goran again and he described a new tension that the team was facing with the local system.

Practice: The promotion of the new manager, who was a certified actuary, was aligned with the norms of London, and of the team. The promotion was based on merit.

Tension: A senior analyst was asked by her family to return to her village. The question then arose, who should fill the vacancy? The team leaders in the UK wanted someone from the team who had proven herself to be capable. The local HR team wanted to promote someone who had completed his or her certification. As Goran explained, "If the hire is based on a certification rather than merit, they will destroy the company asset which we have been building up-a very productive team."

Due to the more demanding work, members of Goran's team had opportunities for competence building, additional responsibility and experience in international collaboration. Employees in the local company frequently made requests to join their team. What team members did not receive, however, was extra time to study for their actuarial exam during work hours, as was possible on other teams. There was simply too much work to do.

With this information in mind, should the promotion be based on merit or qualifications?

"Merit absolutely," emphasized Goran. "If we do not promote our candidate, she will leave and we will lose her experience and knowledge. A big blow to the team." Goran managed the team in India as an extension of the London team and tried to advocate for the London culture.

Qualifications have a great significance in India and indicate that the person has a certain level of knowledge. There are more certified actuaries in London than in Mumbai,[11] so the high number of qualified actuaries in the Indian company gives it some distinction. It is an attractive signal to customers, to prospective employees and to other external stakeholders. The HR team in India were not yet ready to start applying the London norms to their internal promotion practices. Their local market was different.

Resolution: The issue did not settle quietly or quickly. Goran engaged his senior managers in the UK to speak with the senior managers in India and advocate for merit promotion. The India managers resisted the new policy, preferring their own local practices. Over months of discussion and ultimately a trip from the Senior Director in London, they agreed to have an exception and promote based on merit. The team was considered an exception in so many ways and could also be seen as an exception to the cultural norm in this case. In addition, Goran agreed to further support the team members so that they could complete their qualifications.

Goran told these stories not as someone who had conquered the Indian team but as someone who really struggled through the tensions and resolutions. He wondered what he could have done differently so that the first team manager would have stayed. He appreciated the positioning of a London-headquartered company in India and the necessary signals of quality. He was engaged with these tensions, trying to understand, speaking and listening and searching for win-win solutions, even if they were hard to find. Goran did not have these types of tensions when his team was only based in London. These tensions emerge from global virtual teams.

Leading the Embedded Team

This chapter highlights the interconnected and unpredictable nature of virtual teams with team members in different countries. A team leader needs to focus internally, within the team, and also externally for the connection points that can cause friction. A team leader may want to consider the following to support her team.

- The team members will be straddling two cultures, one of the team and the other of the local country. Team members may struggle with this reality, particularly when the cultures are in strong contradiction, which impacts their work or personal circumstances. Be attentive to these dynamics and discuss during one-on-one meetings if possible.

- Develop an adaptive leadership style that engages in what emerges on the team. Prepare yourself to respond to the challenges with the local cultures in a manner that engages conversation, shows respect and seeks comprehensive solutions. Be willing to listen, learn, contribute and adapt.

- As the process toward resolution involves speaking and collaborating with local stakeholders, you may want to build your network of local contacts important to the team. You can begin this while the team is forming, so that when tensions arise, you have already built the personal connections.

- Consider seeking cultural bridges to help you understand the situation. Cultural bridges are people who understand and can articulate the values and assumptions that underlie the cultures and can help you to grasp the deeper underlying issues.

- Recognize that cultural competence is knowing about a culture, and actively engaging to address issues that arise due to the interdependence of the team and the local countries. Cultural competence is also being able to dialogue, listen and creatively resolve tensions with people from other cultures.

Virtual teams create their own team culture with practices and norms. But the unique nature of virtual teams is that the team members are working in different countries. The tensions that arise from this embedded nature can be challenging for the team, and also an amazing opportunity for the team to learn about international and global interconnectedness.

Developing Cultural Competence

In 2010 NTR, the Dutch public service broadcaster, interviewed Yannick Nézet-Séguin, the Principal Conductor of the Rotterdam Philharmonic Orchestra from 2008 to 2018. Nézet-Séguin, originally from Montreal, is a world-renowned conductor and is currently the music director at the Metropolitan Orchestra in New York, Orchestre Métropolitain in Montreal and Philadelphia Orchestra in Philadelphia. He is undeniably a successful global leader.

At the time of the interview, Nézet-Séguin was leading an orchestra of 17 nationalities and traveling the world to perform with other orchestras. The interviewer wanted to know how successful global leaders manage the cultural diversity in their organizations and what business leaders could learn from successful conductors. I show this video when working with global leaders because it is inspiring and practical.

Nézet-Séguin speaks about his experience and reflects on conducting across cultures. Two messages are interesting for this chapter. Firstly, he identified musicians as either more rhythmical or poetic and mentioned the importance of the diversity of approach. "I need to encourage, and not fight against, people who are more rhythmical, even if myself, I am less rhythmical, I prefer something more poetic. But I have to encourage (the diversity) so it makes everything grow, and not to shut it off. And that is very important."

Secondly, when the interviewer asked, "You conduct orchestras all over the world, you even invest time and energy to understand the cultural background?" Nézet-Séguin nodded and replied, "Yes, this is part of my duty, part of my job. I would not conceive this position without this. And I believe now, after a few years of doing it, and having now a dream career… that it has to do very much with this understanding of the backgrounds."

Nézet-Séguin is an example of a culturally competent leader. He understands the benefits of diversity to strengthen ideas and music. He actively encourages the expression of diversity in his team. He learns about the cultures of the countries where his colleagues are from or work. The interviewer was right; there is much that business leaders can learn from successful, culturally competent symphony conductors.

Components of Cultural Competence

A common thread throughout the previous sections of this chapter is cultural competence, meaning the ability to work successfully with people from other cultures. Culturally competent people navigate the geographies easily, engage with people no matter where they are from, and show appropriate signs of respect in ways that are appreciated. As Fons Trompenaars observes, culturally competent people reconcile cultural dilemmas, which begins from a place of deep respect, listening and integration.

Based on the research I have done and my own consulting practice, cultural competence consists of the following four elements:

Knowledge: Understanding of the concepts of culture and how cultural values influence behaviors. Recognition of the different types of knowledge, which includes country-specific facts, cultural values and norms and an appreciation of the more common behaviors in certain situations.

Mindset: An approach to other people with curiosity, openness, ease with uncertainty, growth and humility. A mindset that is inclusive and wants to engage with others from an attitude of respect for who they are and what they have experienced.

Self-Awareness: The ability to be mindful of one's own emotions and thoughts during cultural interactions and respond with respect and compassion. Awareness of one's own cultural preferences and how that impacts other colleagues.

Behavior: Ability to adapt one's behavior to the situation, resolve conflicts that arise from cultural misunderstandings, reconcile cultural dilemmas and be present for the different ways that culture may be expressed during collaborations.

Years ago I had led an acquisition project with stakeholders from many countries. Toward the end of the project, the HR Director praised my performance by saying, "You have the ability to speak with everyone in a way that each needed to hear." It was an important milestone in the development of my own cultural competence.

When I first moved to Europe, I was told that I was too direct, too loud and too 'one size fits all.' In hindsight, the feedback was probably accurate. These observations were made by people from other cultures where these characteristics were not the cultural norm. Coworkers from similar cultures where it was the cultural norm simply shrugged and said "she's fine." In this I recognized that my career in Europe would be limited if I were only able to work with a subset of people. Hence, I worked on my ability to adapt to multicultural work environments. As you can imagine, it has been a long and exciting journey.

A key moment for learning about cultures results from culture clashes, when different ways of communicating and collaborating lead to a conflict. The people involved may react in many ways, such as anger, frustration, withdrawal, sadness or disbelief. All of these reactions stem from the internal question, 'What is happening here?' A natural first reaction is to wonder why the other people involved are acting like they are. Another way to view the interaction is to wonder why you are acting like you are. What does the culture clash incident say about you, your preferences and how you have been influenced by your culture?

Through this reflective process, people can realize the way their view of acceptable values, norms and behaviors has been influenced by the culture(s) where they were raised. They then have the chance to expand what they know to be acceptable and take on new ways of being.

Developing cultural competence takes time, relies on experience and experimentation and accelerates with helpful feedback. Forty years ago, only well-traveled executives and expats had the need and opportunity to develop cultural competence. They were immersed in a country and could see, smell, taste and touch the various unique qualities of the cultural environment. Now many people throughout the organization need to develop cultural competence and must do so even while they remain in their own country.

Developing Cultural Competence Virtually

It is possible to develop cultural competence virtually, and virtual team members benefit when teams intentionally dedicate time and energy toward that endeavor. Following are ideas for developing cultural competence on your team:

- **Discuss Culture as a Team:** Actively encourage and schedule times when team members speak about their countries and the latest events there. Ask team members to facilitate conversations on topics that shed light on different perspectives within the team. Topics might include different educational systems, what happens when you visit a customer, how you greet your colleagues in the morning and so on. Facilitate questions to understand the values behind the cultural practices.

- **Team Trainings:** Cultural trainings can have a positive impact on the development of cultural competence of the individual and of the team as a whole. An effective trainer can help the team to understand the topic more deeply, to bring awareness of how culture impacts the team's collaboration and to facilitate critical conversations that build bridges and trust. Over the years, I have noticed that the best timing for a training is actually a few months after the team has already started working together. They are usually still at the point where they like and respect each other, but they are starting to experience concrete problems that can be unpacked in the workshop. This puts the team on the right path for future cross-border collaboration.

- **Leader as the Role Model:** Team members benefit by having a culturally competent leader. It gives them a concrete example of the mindset and behaviors that build bridges and foster collaboration. Also, a leader helps to create a team culture that values diversity and encourages team norms to integrate differences. Team leaders have an enormous influence on the attitudes of the team members and can foster a spirit of inclusiveness.

- **Team Reflection:** Schedule time for the team to reflect on the question of how the team is doing as a multicultural team. Depending on the psychological safety within the team, and their willingness to share, you may need to provide different ways to answer this question, such as during a virtual video meeting or anonymously in a survey. Take time out to focus on *how* the team is working, communicating and collaborating together.

- **Support Individual Development:** Some team members may find working internationally difficult because they will often feel out of their comfort zone. Help them to experiment, review their experience and provide a supportive environment to develop. Remember, learning about other cultures while staying in one's own country can be more challenging because they miss the visuals, sounds and tangible artifacts of another culture.

- **Contact Intensity:** Alfred Presbitero from Deankin University and Lemuel S. Toledano of CanPLAY Pty Ltd measured the impact of cultural trainings on the cultural intelligence and performance of virtual teams.[12] Learning about cultures alone can already positively impact the performance of a multicultural team.

    Interestingly, they found that post-training 'contact intensity' played a role in the effectiveness of the cultural trainings. They defined contact intensity as the "team member's assessment of his or her level of communication, interaction, and engagement with other team members." I define contact intensity as lively team meetings, interesting conversations that go beyond the tasks at hand, and friendly chat sessions that celebrate team and personal milestones.

Successful global virtual teams need culturally competent people to realize the potential the diversity of thought and experience in the team offers. Developing cultural competence includes learning through research and books, conversations with other colleagues and experiences that push one's personal boundaries. Throughout, though, developing cultural competence deepens with self-awareness and reflection, especially of one's emotional responses during cultural interactions and of one's own cultural preferences.

Learning from a Distance - Inspiration

Joyci is a delightful Brazilian woman, bubbling with kindness and smiles. During our virtual interview, her daughter came into the room to kiss her goodbye on the way to school. Joyci has attended formal cultural training workshops and her team leader supports the development of cultural competence amongst team members. Joyci's opinion on the virtual experience demonstrates the possibilities for people who work virtually. "I have been with the company about 16 years, and I have always had my boss and colleagues sitting near me. About two years ago we changed the structure of the organization and suddenly my boss was not sitting beside me anymore. And we became responsible for the Americas, so we moved from a Latin culture to an expanded type of culture, interacting with colleagues from the US, who are more demanding and straight forward. We also work with the colleagues in Sweden, in China, and in Thailand. The world expanded suddenly and it was really an amazing experience.

"I have two responsibilities - a global and local position at the same time. I currently most enjoy working in the global, multicultural environment, as opposed to working here with my Brazilian colleagues. Because I still have a lot of things to learn, because I have some struggle points with some cultures, and as you see I speak with lots of energy, and so I need to mold myself to act differently in different places, and this is something that I am learning. I see more clearly the way that the things happen here, like respecting the time of others, or leading people from different cultures. I see how much you can learn and that there is not a right or wrong, but it is the way it is. Also, sometimes you learn, sometimes you teach."

Learning through Multicultural Collaboration: An Example

A key message through this book is that global collaborations provide a rich opportunity for learning and personal development. Many people ask 'What should I do?' when faced with a culture clash that is impacting their ability to work with remote colleagues. Let's use an example based on a true, and very common, story.

A multinational company was headquartered in the Netherlands and had subsidiaries around the world, including a shared services center in India. Many Dutch and Indian colleagues struggled to work well together. I will use fictitious names to tell the story: Jan from the Netherlands and Sarthak from India. Here are their respective points of view:

Jan: Sarthak was not forthcoming as to whether he could complete the work on time. Jan would send an email to request work to be completed by a certain time. He expected a 'yes' or a 'no' response. Jan said that Sarthak always answered 'yes,' but the work was not always done on time. This would put Jan in an awkward situation concerning planning. If Sarthak had responded with a 'no,' Jan could have found an alternative.

Sarthak: Jan did not create a positive working relationship. They hardly knew each other, and Sarthak had never seen Jan on video camera. Most of their communication was via email and, according to Sarthak, very unfriendly, with only the details of the request. Sarthak hardly knew anything about his colleague.

When Sarthak received a request from Jan, two things went through his head. He wanted to show respect to his colleague, and he wanted to fulfill the request. To say 'no' to Jan's request would have been disrespectful in Sarthak's mind, particularly to someone he hardly knew and who was located in the headquarters.

In addition, Sarthak believed there is always a way to get things done. He would read Jan's request and think, 'This must be possible!' even if he did not possess the know-how and skill set at that moment. He would brainstorm with his colleagues, put in extra hours, do whatever it took to try to complete the assignment. For these two reasons, he would not say 'no' to Jan.

Jan: Generally time spent on social talk was a waste of time. His goal was to write very clear email requests so that Sarthak did not have any doubts about the assignment. Jan considered video calls to be exceptions and believed that email was a sufficient communication tool.

When I spoke with each of them separately, it was clear that they hardly knew each other. Due to the setup of the request process, their relationship was very transactional, and yet, cultural assumptions seeped in so that both Jan and Sarthak were frustrated.

In this example, there is no right or wrong person. Jan and Sarthak are both behaving in ways that are culturally acceptable to their respective locations. How can they go beyond the way they think they should behave and incorporate new assumptions and behaviors?

Step 1: Each person examines their own reactions and reflects upon what that says about their own assumptions about acceptable behavior. This is not an easy task because it is like asking a fish to describe water. Jan and Sarthak can speak with colleagues and reference books or other resources to gain insight into what drives their own expectations.

Step 2: With a curious mindset, research the other country. The behavior that each of them witnesses is only a small piece of the whole culture. Both Jan and Sarthak are trying to understand why the behaviors they observe make sense for their colleague.

Step 3: Have a conversation together about each other's way of working in a manner that is respectful and open. If they think of solutions right away, then they have missed the deeper learning from each other. Treat the conversation as an inquiry.

Step 4: Agree a way of working together where they both benefit. In this example, I suggest a solution in which they are both out of their comfort zones but also grow beyond their strict cultural norms. Jan learns the importance of creating a relationship with Sarthak, and they agree to have a weekly video call. Within that trusting relationship, Sarthak becomes more forthcoming with how he thinks about the task request; for instance, can he do it easily, or is this new type of work. They both help each other. Sarthak encourages Jan to turn on the video and share non-work information, and Jan encourages Sarthak to examine a task more practically.

In parallel, they are both learning about the other's country. For instance, watching movies, reading books by local authors and following the local news. Their worlds have expanded through this collaboration.

Developing cultural competence happens through culture shock events. Our first reaction may be 'they are impossible to work with,' but we can use the conflict to learn and grow. Here's a clue: 'we are also impossible to work with.' Through self-reflection, curiosity, dialogue and integration, the impossible becomes possible and enjoyable.

Key Points

- Culture impacts virtual teams in 3 ways which are different than co-located teams.
- The first way culture impacts a multicultural virtual team is *within the team*. Colleagues from diverse cultures may communicate, make decisions, build trust and other team processes differently.
- The second way culture impacts the virtual team is *between the locations*. Team members may think abstractly of their distant colleagues and may rely on cultural stereotypes to create subgroups.
- The third way culture impacts the team is *outside of the team.* Although the team creates its own norms and processes, each team member is located in a local culture which may affect the team.
- Even though team members are sitting in their own countries, they

may experience cultural dynamics as they work on a virtual team with their culturally diverse colleagues.

- While learning about other cultures, team members have the opportunity to also learn about themselves and their own cultural preferences. This ability to self-reflect is critical for developing cultural competence.
- Virtual team members need to develop cultural competence even though they may never leave their own country. The team leader could support this development within the team.

Part Two: Attitudes and Levers

CHAPTER 4

Attitudes and Beliefs

In 2014, Google completed Project Aristotle, a two-year internal study of 180 Google teams.[1] They wanted to use their exceptional data-driven analytical techniques to determine what made some teams thrive and others drown, especially those teams involved in innovation, creativity and change. In the end, the study put the spotlight on psychological safety, a critical element in the workplace, and which I cover later in this book.

Another interesting finding of the study was that the same people could work on multiple teams together, and yet they would experience each team differently. One person in a morning meeting with one team will have a different feeling and experience in an afternoon meeting with another team, even if many of the team members are the same. This means that each team has created an atmosphere unique to that team, and this atmosphere ultimately impacts performance and satisfaction. I focused a microscope on the team atmosphere for virtual teams to discern what this might mean for team leaders.

The results are noteworthy. In the CALDO model, I call this aspect of cooperation *attitudes and beliefs*. By this, I refer to what team members think and feel about the team and their colleagues. Is this a team with high levels of trust? Do they feel like they belong or are they disengaged? Do they feel psychologically safe to express their opinions, even if the opinions are different from everyone else's?

In academic literature, these team attitudes are called *emergent states,* meaning that they arise from *how* the team works together and reflect the quality of the team environment. The objectives of two different teams may be the same, but *how* they complete the work can be very different. For instance, one team may have a few people who dominate the infrequent meetings based on their expertise. They mostly use email and rarely use chat. Another team may use a variety of communication tools for both formal and informal topics. They share information easily, use positive and encouraging words and speak equally during meetings. If you were to attend the meetings or read the posts of each of these teams, you would very quickly sense the contrast, and conversations with the team members would further confirm the vast differences in how they feel about each team.

Time and again, research proves that team climate can impact the performance of the team, especially in the long run. The correlation, however, is not causal. Just because a team feels a high level of trust doesn't mean that performance will automatically increase. However, because the team has high trust, they are able to share information quickly and rely on each other for decisions. The resulting speed and efficiency of decision-making can translate into higher performance.

The CALDO model has arrows going from team *attitudes and beliefs* back to the *teamwork.* It shows how the emergent states are formed and how it can impact performance through working together.

This chapter will help you understand key elements of a virtual team climate, how it is formed and how it impacts performance. With this information, you can measure your own team climate and assess where your team is thriving and where it may need support.

Trust

Trust is one of the most researched topics on virtual teams because it is fundamental to the success of the team. Professors Breur, Hüffmeier and Hertel in their paper in which the title began "Does Trust Matter More in Virtual Teams?…" examined studies about trust and virtual teams and found higher trust correlated with higher performance.[2] When team members trust each other, they will share information, cover for each other, resolve conflicts more easily, ask for help and have an open approach with the team. Given the increased risks on virtual teams, trust correlated very positively with high team performance, even more so than for co-located teams.

Hence, the next question is how to build trust in a virtual team. As we learn throughout this book, it is different from building trust amongst a co-located team.

Types of Trust

"Ach, I really don't trust him" is an often-heard phrase. When someone says that they do not trust a colleague, it can be very difficult to understand why the trust is missing. The answer could range from a shrug of the shoulders and a simple "It's just how I feel" to a long list of offensives committed by the presumed untrustworthy person. This is because trust is a broad concept that impacts our minds and our feelings.

Generally, there are three types of trust:

Relationship Trust is built upon how I consider you as a person. Perhaps we have things in common, which is the basis for the development of a bond, and I learn that you are someone I consider to have integrity, generosity and kindness. I have warm feelings for you.

Capability Trust means that I consider you to be able to complete the task, and that you are competent in your roles and responsibilities. You have the background and have shown yourself to be someone whom I could trust to do the work. This trust is usually context specific. I may trust Glen with the delivery of the engineering drawings but not to operate on my heart.

Reliability Trust means that I can turn to you in times of crisis and you have my back, so to speak. When plans do not go as expected, you will respond quickly and competently to help. Also, I can rely on you to be loyal to me when speaking with others.

Part of trust comes from the head and part from the heart. All trust is trying to fill the space of vulnerability so that a person can put his attention elsewhere. When a team member is not sure if a colleague can and will do the agreed task, he can be preoccupied with doubt, and that negatively affects overall performance.

Trust between Team Members

How do team members build trust in each other? Let's first consider a co-located team.

Imagine a new project on a co-located team. Some of the team know each other already and some are completely new. The team goes to lunch together to kick off the project. As they begin sharing personal information, they realize that some of them like the same sports team, some have children in the same school and some like to ski at the same ski resort on the weekend. They start to make personal connections.

In addition, when a team member explains his professional background, the other team members likely will know the universities, the associations and the companies. They begin to develop trust in a colleague's qualifications through an appreciation for the professional references.

Finally, the team members show interest with physical gestures such as sitting nearby, turning to each other and the friendly handshake or bow.

Now imagine a virtual team. Attempts to find commonalities between team members falls flat. Their worlds are different. Two colleagues may both have kids, but they do not attend the same school. Some others may both like football, but most likely do not support the same team. In a co-located team, shared interests are on a more personal and detailed level. On a virtual team, shared interests are more abstract and less personal level.

When team members share their professional references, it often results in a blank stare from their new colleagues. Without knowing the universities or professional organizations to which the colleague refers, the virtual team cannot confirm the trustworthiness of or rank the qualifications of their new colleague.

Finally, the physical gestures to show interest are limited to those within the confines of the video screen.

Swift Trust to Deep Trust

Researchers have identified an interesting phenomenon that occurs when people work together.[3] They call it 'swift trust,' which is the temporary trust in another's competences and dependability. Team members begin at a position of trusting the other. This is one of the reasons why short-term projects can be successful. The swift trust carries the team members to the end of the collaboration.

On longer cooperations, swift trust must quickly be replaced by real trust, and in a virtual team this is developed through working together.

As the team works together, they start to exhibit personal and professional characteristics. Team members show they are reliable, committed to the team, capable in the tasks, supportive, responsive, etc. As the team members continue to collaborate, they have the chance to communicate about themselves, and build social closeness and trust, which can positively impact their performance.

To summarize, virtual teams begin with swift trust, quickly replace this with capability trust when they work together and over time build relationship and reliability trust.

Benefits of Trust vs Costs of Collaboration

Imagine that you as a team leader have one task that requires two people and one of the experts is Sandra, in London. Your choice for the second person is either Henry, also in London, or Boris, in Moscow, and each is equally competent. Whom should you assign to work with Sandra?

If you want to minimize the costs of collaboration, you would assign Sandra and Henry. Collaboration costs on a virtual team are the extra efforts necessary when working with someone, including the use of technology, time zones or cultural differences. In general, this would mean that a local colleague, all things being equal, would be more desirable on a task than a remote colleague.

However, if you are thinking of building trust in the team, and how swift trust turns into real trust through interdependence on tasks, then you would consider that Sandra and Boris work together. This may seem counterintuitive on a virtual team. In the absence of informal interaction and chats at the coffee machine, which would normally build relationship trust, working together interdependently becomes the trust builder itself. Once the trust in the team has been established, then you can organize task assignments with less interdependence and thus less collaboration costs.

Although I am suggesting for remote colleagues to work together, this does not mean that conversations are only about work. Through working together, the teams have the chance to have conversations to learn about each other, communicate regularly and build the relationship trust.

Trust Me, I'm Management

The starting point for examining trust in a team is the team leader. Look at yourself in the mirror. Are you a trustworthy person? This is a tough question to answer. Are you reliable, competent and dependable? Are you a person of integrity? Trust in the team leader can impact the trust levels throughout the whole team.

Every team member has different expectations of the leader. Often people will test you to see if you are trustworthy, and they may do so in different ways. I recall a situation between a Chinese and a Swedish colleague, Hai and Sven, respectively. They had been working together for six months when Sven traveled to China to meet Hai, which would be their second time meeting in person. When Hai saw the very fit and trim Sven, he said, "Ah, I see you have gained weight." Such a personal observation amongst coworkers in Sweden, particularly one that is negative, would be considered inappropriate as well as rude. But when Hai told me the story, he said, "I was testing Sven. If he responded with a shrug of the shoulders and a fun comment, then I knew that we were connected enough as people for trust, that we have intimacy. If he was offended, then I would have to continue working on the relationship as we would not have reached a trusting level yet." Luckily, Sven laughed off Hai's comment, and the trust Hai imagined was confirmed.

Team leaders may not always be conscious of it, but team members often look for signs of trust in their team leader, particularly those who are far away. The following section outlines some examples of signals that can build trustworthiness, even from a distance.[4]

Empathy: Most team members want to know that the team leader understands their working conditions, as well as their challenges and their priorities. They want to know that their team leader is ready to help them succeed within their unique situation and that the leader cares about their issues.

Perceived Justice: Team members want fairness. They trust leaders who treat all team members with respect and who avoid showing bias or favoritism within the team. Team members also want to believe that their team leader is making decisions that are fair, and often this means that the team leader needs to explain how and why she made decisions. For example, how and why the team members were assigned their tasks, or how and why funding was allocated across the team. The important underlying message is that decisions were made fairly.

Accessibility: Most team members want to know that the team leader is available when they need them. This does not mean a 24/7 hotline, but they need to know when they will be able to get the leader's attention. For example, the team member is more content when she knows that her email or text communication to a team leader will be answered in a timely manner, such as on the next working day.

Trust Across Cultures

Imagine a team of Chinese and Dutch colleagues. How would each culture build trust? Interestingly, a team of researchers in China, UK and the Netherlands found differences between the two cultures.[5]

The Dutch teams assumed that their colleagues were open and benevolent, meaning that they easily shared information and supported each other. They judged the trustworthiness of a person based on whether that person is competent, has the knowledge and skills and will perform to the standard.

In contrast to the Dutch team, the Chinese teams assumed that everyone is competent and honest, which is a reflection of a person's character, integrity and authenticity. They judged trustworthiness based on the openness of a colleague, such as whether they are sharing information at work and sharing personal stories of their lives, as a proxy for the quality of the relationship. A strong personal relationship is critical for Chinese people to work together. If team members are not open with each other, the business relationship will suffer.

	Dutch	Chinese
Assume a person has these characteristics	Open, benevolent, share information, support each other	Competence, honesty
Identify and exhibit these characteristics to build trust	Competence, knowledge and skills	Open, share information, share personal stories

This presents a paradox in a virtual team of Chinese and Dutch colleagues. The Dutch will focus on their competence to show they are trustworthy, whereas the Chinese will look for signs of openness. The Chinese will focus on being open and building relationships by spending time together with colleagues, whereas the Dutch will look for signs of competence. Mixed signals and different priorities will lead both sides of the team to say "I don't trust them!"

Fixing the Paradox

What can a leader do to help develop the teams cultural competence so that they understand what is happening? The leader can include cultural diversity as a topic in regular meetings and coach the team members to learn new ways of building trust and showing trustworthy behavior. The team may also benefit from attending a cultural competence course together and discussing their different assumptions about trust. Through this collaboration, the team members have the opportunity to develop new ways to interact across cultures.

Psychological Safety

The news of Google's research on their own teams took the learning and organizational development community by storm when it was revealed that Google had found the key distinguishing feature of successful teams.[6] In a two-year long initiative, which they called Project Aristotle, Google researchers studied the details of their teams. They surveyed, interviewed, observed and evaluated data and referenced years of research on teams. In the end, they identified the differentiator for successful teams at Google. It can all be summed up as *psychological safety*. How a person feels in a team environment will have an impact on the performance of the entire team.

Although psychological safety was first identified in the 1960s, Professor Amy Edmundson at Harvard has shown the business public the importance of psychological safety through her own research and books. She defines psychological safety as:

The perceptions of the consequences of taking interpersonal risks in a particular context such as a workplace.[7]

A psychologically safe environment exists when team members feel that they can share their opinions, express themselves, ask questions and contribute ideas without the risk of embarrassment, loss of face or other disrespectful responses. The negative responses trigger our instinctive 'fight or flight' mode. When we perceive a threat or feel unsafe, the amygdala in our brain turns on our survival instincts, thereby shutting off any other more reasonable brain functions. We are not feeling safe, even if the threat is not a lion or a bear, but our own reputation, feelings of competence or feelings of belonging.

Why would Google find that this is *the key differentiator*? Professor Edmondson, Google and other researchers have found that psychological safety has an impact on performance in the following ways:

Innovation increases due to different points of view being voiced and heard. Diverse teams are more likely to leverage their unique perspectives in a psychologically safe environment.

Decision quality improves when everyone has a chance to express contra views that inevitably reduce the risk of 'group think.' A quick test to determine whether a team feels psychologically safe is to ask, 'does everyone on the team feel that they can voice an opinion that is different from the rest of the team?'

Team learning improves as new ideas from outside the team are welcomed and expressed within the team.

Information sharing improves as the team embrace task conflict and feel welcome to express their point of view.

As you can imagine, psychological safety is also a critical ingredient on virtual teams.

Professors Gibson and Gibbs of University of California Irvine and Rutgers University, respectively, examined virtual teams and the characteristics that blocked innovative thinking.[8] They identified that distance, technology, cultural diversity and the tendency for higher turnover negatively impact the ability of virtual teams to innovate. And yet, it is often the virtual, international teams that companies most expect and need to innovate. After all, they have access to talent and diverse information sources, which enables them to be cutting edge. Are these virtual teams doomed by the characteristics of their existence?

No, said the professors. Psychological safety makes the difference. They surveyed and interviewed businesspeople in companies who belong to teams with measurable objectives and deliverables. When these diverse, multi-location teams had psychological safety, they were able to innovate.

Gibson and Gibbs wrote the following about psychological safety and cultural diversity: "…a psychologically safe communication climate helped raise and clarify differences in national orientations and norms, resolve conflict, and foster an open environment in which team members felt comfortable to ask questions, admit to a lack of understanding and voice opinions. This increased innovation by allowing different perspectives and viewpoints to be heard, enabling the merging of ideas and helping to establish a middle ground and bridge differences."

Creating Psychological Safety in Virtual Teams

As a team leader, you may be looking for answers on how to create psychological safety within your virtual, multicultural team. Psychological safety does not mean teams avoid confrontation or disagreements. In fact, in a psychologically safe team, disagreements are encouraged, mistakes are discussed and analyzed and failure is a chance to learn. Here are some ideas that may apply to your team:

- Facilitate a conversation in the team about psychological safety. Start by building awareness of the benefits of a psychologically safe team culture and how their words and actions can contribute. Start with a survey (perhaps the first is anonymous) to measure the current level of psychological safety in the team and explore how to improve if necessary.
- Develop cultural competence within the team. Team members need to develop the knowledge and competence to communicate in ways that are inclusive. They can avoid unconscious, disrespectful words that lead to a psychological shut down or cause doubt in others.
- Measure the amount of time each person speaks during a meeting. Teams in which team members have equal speaking time tend to feel more psychologically safe. Actively facilitate the discussions so that everyone has a chance to share their ideas.

- Encourage discussions of different viewpoints on task conflict. Try to emphasize that differences in opinion are an opportunity to synergize. Help people to accept the uneasiness while searching for a new idea together.
- Avoid words that blame, criticize or shut down ideas. Team members in a country may say something that is completely unusual for you and completely normal for them. Use words that open up conversation to explore more deeply everyone's suggestions.
- View mistakes as an opportunity to learn. Thank the persons who have admitted the errors and use the lessons learned to improve the future.
- Look at yourself as a leader and manager. How do you handle stress, mistakes, failures and the time-consuming discussions in the team? Would you feel psychologically safe in your own team?

Example of low psychological safety in a virtual team

Celeste prepared for a video meeting with a six-person engineering team. They were at a critical moment in the project because they needed to choose between two proposed technologies in this meeting. They had been exchanging emails and sharing documents, but every time the team came together to discuss the topic, the team leader, Suhail, and the engineer, Dan, completely dominated the discussions. Dan had the most experience with Technology A, and clearly favored that as the solution. The other team members had perspectives on Technologies A and B, but they were not sharing their experience.

Generally, Suhail would run the meeting and would sometimes ask, "Anyone have anything to add?" which was met with dead silence. In truth, Suhail was glad to just get through the meeting as quickly as possible. He knew that meetings without discussions were a waste of time, but he just did not know what to do about it.

At the moment in the meeting when the team was about to make a decision, Dan immediately voiced his preference for Technology A. "Anyone have a different opinion?" asked Suhail. Hesitantly, Celeste started to speak, "Yes, I would like to also consider technology B," she began. As she started to list some of the advantages, Dan made disapproving sounds and finally said, "Sorry Celeste, but you do not really understand how the technology works. I have had experience, and most of your points are not realized if we select Technology B."

At that point Celeste became silent. She waited for Suhail to facilitate the discussion and to comment on both Dan's statement and his behavior. Instead, Suhail said, "In the interest of time, and given Dan's experience, let's select Technology A. Anyone disagree?" There was silence on the line. "Good, I will propose Technology A to the Steering Committee. Let's move on to the last topic on the agenda," Suhail rushed ahead. And with that, he lost Celeste's commitment to the team because she did not feel psychologically safe. She thought to herself, "Let's get this over with and stop wasting my time." Since she could not share her opinion with the team, she decided that she would tell her country manager, who was on the Steering Committee, and who did listen carefully.

Suhail was later surprised by how much resistance there was from the Steering Committee against the proposal. He had to spend a lot of time reworking the proposal and further investigating different solutions. This delayed the project and left him feeling frustrated.

This familiar scenario shows a remote team with low psychological safety. What were the clues? Dan dominated and Suhail did nothing about it. Celeste tried to speak but was cut off. The rest of the team remained silent, which Suhail interpreted as agreement.

Suhail did not effectively try to solicit other opinions. Since the team did not have an in-depth conversation amongst themselves, other stakeholders outside the team became involved.

Shared Team Identity

When I started my career, I belonged to the finance department. In the morning, we all went through the same door to the building, we all saw the same signs about company values and we all went up the stairs to our location in the building. Our desks were in the same area, which was where the finance people sat. We had family photos on our desks, and we asked each other "How are you today?" to get a feel of the mood.

As members of the department, we discussed our shared goals and what we wanted to accomplish for the year and we assigned tasks. As we tried to reach these goals, we helped each other, filled in when someone was sick or struggling and we all shared information that might be relevant. We went to lunch together regularly, and every so often we went to the local bar for Friday night Happy Hour. Some of us even played on the company volleyball team and called ourselves the Finance Fine.

We had visual cues, location cues and interaction cues that reminded us that we were a team. We were the finance department, which contrasted to the sales department. We knew who was in our department and who was not.

These cues helped us to form a team identity, which is a powerful cognitive and emotional binding factor for a team. On virtual teams, the visual, location and rhythmic cues (such as lunch together) disappear. Yet virtual teams want and need the benefits of a team identity, the feeling that they are a member of something bigger than themselves and to which they want to contribute their best.

A team identity reflects whether a team member feels connected with the others, thinks of the team as being part of their own personal identity and behaves in a way that supports the sustainability of the team. Team members would be more likely to express sentiments such as "I feel proud to belong to this team" or "I am energized by the work we do together."

Virtual team members who identity with the team tend to behave in ways that positively impact team performance, such as:

Shared team identity minimizes conflict between virtual team members. When team members feel connected by a common identity, they interpret the behavior of others more positively and will informally reach out and communicate to resolve misunderstandings before they escalate.

Team members who identify with a team engage in behavior that prioritizes the welfare of the team over other groups or their own self-interest. They will put in extra efforts to move the team forward.

Shared team identity can bridge the subgroup identities formed by location (see section Between the Locations in Chapter Three). By emphasizing the common values and norms of the virtual team, team members are more willing to collaborate with each other.

In the zeal to create a team identity, the virtual team leader may face some realities that need to be considered.

People belong to multiple teams. The flexibility of virtual work and the global reach of responsibilities may well contribute to an increase in the number of teams to which people belong. Colleagues are members of their department team, their country team, the business unit team, all the project teams and the knowledge center team, just to name a few. Their identity with one team, and particularly yours, may be less strong.

Conflicting team goals. As team members belong to multiple teams, they can have KPIs and goals that are in conflict with each other. When this happens, team members will struggle to put their best efforts into the one team.

Team membership is fluid. Who is in and who is out of the team changes more fluidly in a virtual team. Often teams will identify core team members, and then those who are 'as needed,' when their expertise, network or advice is relevant. Who is core and who is not may change over the life of a project team, which could be confusing for all team members as well as other stakeholders.

Amount of necessary collaboration changes over time. Team members may begin working independently, happy in their own locations and sharing information every so often. Then a phase may begin whereby they need to work together, changing how they view each other and their contribution to the team. Some team members struggle with the transition to an increased level of interaction, even though they have always been a team member.

Shared team identity plays an important function on a high-performance team. The visible communication cues on co-located teams are not available on virtual teams. The nature of virtual teams makes a shared team identity even more essential for the team's success. In the absence of the communication cues, virtual teams need to intentionally develop the shared team identity.

Below are effective suggestions to build the identity and spirit for the virtual team.

Team purpose, goals and norms: A compelling and clear shared purpose, objectives, team norms and a team charter define and set the boundaries of the team.

Team symbols and visuals: As virtual teams miss so many visual cues, creative and meaningful symbols can help team members feel a sense of cohesiveness with their remote colleagues. A team name and symbol in particular act as a uniting force, a reminder that the team member belongs to a team.

Informal communication: Professors P. Hinds and M. Mortensen found that informal communication strengthens the shared team identity.[9] The phone call, scheduled coffee break or quick text to say hello help build bonds between team members.

Regularly repeat the team kick-off events: The transient nature of virtual teams can result in loose connections that need to be strengthened. When teams have kick-off events, they often introduce team members, discuss shared purpose and objectives and spend time building the team. Virtual teams can make these one-off events a regular occurrence corresponding to the changes in team membership.

Celebrate individual and team success: Often teams focus on task completion and quickly move on. It is nice to check things off, but the feeling of completion through celebration can help the team to bond together. For instance, recognizing milestones, over-the-top performance and effective team collaboration.

One-on-one meetings: In the interviews and conversations with various leaders and team members, I found that team members highly appreciate the one-on-one meetings with the team leader. The agendas of these regular (for instance biweekly) meetings are set by the team members and generally do not include task-related topics. Topics often include mentoring, coaching and career development advice. Team members value these sessions because they feel that they are receiving attention for their unique situation, even from a distance.

Recognize birthdays, local holidays, personal celebrations: It helps within the team to share the special events of each person. Often virtual teams include global team members in different local customs and holidays, which can be celebrated together.

Team Building for Team Identity

Nathalie is a successful Regional HR Director of a multinational manufacturer. She is smart and energetic, and someone you could approach at a networking event, a people person. Her department had people in three locations-Berlin, Paris and Lisbon. She wanted to create a team feeling, but they were only allowed to meet once per year. We brainstormed on how she could create the team spirit, and she ultimately implemented a fun exercise with her team.

"I decided to organize virtual team building days," she explained. "Originally, I wanted once a month, but in reality it was once every two months. We would all take off on a Friday afternoon and do the same thing but in our own locations. For instance, on the first Friday, we all went to a yoga center in our own cities and had a yoga lesson. We would send pictures and video with each other and create some spirit from the activity. We were all laughing together. On Monday morning we would have a video meeting and share some more. The next time on a Friday, we all went to learn to cook, but again in our own cities. Sharing photos, videos, all that stuff. Seeing what each other were doing. It was great fun and really worked! Over time we didn't do it as much, but in the beginning, it really made a difference to building the team." Periodically I met some of the people in Nathalie's department, and they all confirmed that it was a great way to build the team from a distance. They smiled while recalling the yoga positions.

Nathalie's ingenious approach worked because of two concepts coming together: *self-identification* and *social identification*.

Self-identification means that an individual feels like a unique and valued person in the team. Social identification means a person identifies with the group. These concepts seem to be opposing, but they are two sides of the same coin. In team identity, we need both the recognition as a unique individual and a feeling of inclusiveness in the group.

In Nathalie's story, the team members shared similar experiences and felt like they were part of a team. This led to an identity that built on a social connection.

At the same time, the team members were in their own locations, showing how they do things and feeling recognized for their contribution to the fun.

Often in a virtual team, both the social identify and the individual identity are hijacked by a focus on the meeting agendas and tasks at hand. These extra efforts, even from a distance, can help everyone to feel like a team.

Key Points

- Virtual teams begin with swift trust, but this must quickly be replaced by actual trust based on reliability and competence. Over time, team members then build relationship trust.
- One way to build trust if for team members to work together across locations, interdependently.

- Virtual team leaders show they are trustworthy by being empathetic, accessible and fair.
- Psychological safety is necessary for multicultural virtual teams who want to leverage the cultural diversity for innovation.
- Teams who actively create a shared team identity can help the team members to feel connected even though they may identify with their local organizations.
- Team leaders should actively support the team to create a shared team identity both in the beginning and throughout the life of the team.
- When a team is not performing as expected, the team leader should examine whether the team members trust each other, whether they feel safe to express themselves and whether they identify with the team.

Leadership Levers

When I finish explaining to a team how cultural diversity impacts virtual teams and why virtual teams are different than co-located, I inevitably am asked the question, 'Then what should we do?' Whomever has asked this question realizes that the methods they have learned to lead a co-located team will be insufficient for a virtual team. They are genuinely open and curious to know how they can lead in the multicultural virtual context.

The lack of physical presence changes the landscape for the team. The team leader cannot walk by the colleague's desk, the team cannot enjoy a project kick-off lunch and the colleagues cannot meet each other in the hallway. But the team leader still wants what these actions supported, namely, the oversight that work is progressing, the team spirit and cohesion and the up-to-date information sharing. In the virtual team, they are possible but in a different way.

To answer the question, I identified four Leadership Levers based on the teams I met in my consulting practice, the research I found in academia and the virtual leaders I interviewed. I noticed that the activities that the successful team leaders and teams did were multifaceted. They organized themselves to achieve their goals, just like any team, but unlike co-located teams, they had to do so while rarely seeing each other in person. What seems obvious on a co-located team when everyone experiences the same environment needed to be intentionally developed when the team members were remote.

The four Leadership Levers of the CALDO model are:

I. Eliminate Uncertainty. Team members arrive in their new teams with many questions and doubts, which can be answered. For instance, who are my team members? How will we work together?

II. Create the Team. As the team leader cannot be everywhere, the team itself plays a more prominent role to drive the progress.

III. Bring in the Humanity. The nature of the technology and distance encourages a focus on tasks and separation at the expense of human connection, a crucial foundation for team success and creativity.

IV. Complete the Work. The team achieves deliverables and celebrates success while located remotely and using various technologies.

In the CALDO model, the Levers are the actions that ultimately impact the quality of teamwork and the quality of the attitudes and determine whether the team achieve the outcomes. For instance, the time spent to create a team will impact the quality of the shared team identity, which will determine whether team members share information and support each other, thereby impacting teamwork quality and outcomes. All these elements are integrated in the holistic CALDO model.

CHAPTER 5

Eliminating Uncertainty

It can be intimidating when someone first joins a virtual team. He receives an email with a list of the names, job titles, email addresses and possibly pictures of his colleagues, along with a calendar invitation for an introduction meeting with the team leader. Questions buzz through his head. Who are these people? What is my role? How will we work together? Where are they located? Will we succeed together or is this the end of my career? He looks at his cold black computer and longs for the warm fuzzy welcome he used to receive from his local teams.

This type of uncertainty can cause stress. This section of the book, the first Leadership Lever, is an appeal to the team leader to eliminate the so-called 'unknown knowns,' which refers to those things that are knowable but are not yet known when the team is first assembled. 'Unknown knowns' include roles and responsibilities, team member personalities, aspects of the different cultures and how the team will work together. It is important for team development and work quality to address these topics while clarifying the team goals and objectives.

This chapter is about taking the time to decrease the uncertainty levels in the virtual team, and this will help your team members feel the level of comfort they need to operate at their best.

Roles and Responsibilities

Members of virtual teams are often very busy people-on multiple teams, often in a matrix organization with multiple stakeholders. Defining the roles and responsibilities is critical for all teams, but even more so on virtual teams because they do not have the informal, hallway conversations to keep them motivated.

Team members want to know why they are on the team and the expectations of their contributions. In addition, the other team members are wondering why the others are on the team as well. The process of defining roles and responsibilities brings clarity for everyone.

Team Collaboration: How the Team Works Together

When my Dutch husband and I (American) agreed to marry, I soon realized that to marry was the only thing we agreed upon. We had different ideas of who should organize the wedding, how the day should progress and the number of ceremonies we would have. We each had a design based on the 'normal' practices in each of our countries.

This phenomenon also happens on global virtual teams. Each person arrives with assumptions of what they consider 'normal' working procedures. Once they start working with someone who has a different definition of 'normal,' uncertainty often increases, as well as frustrations and complaints.

I have described the three types of conflict in the section titled Conflict. One of the detrimental types of conflict for a team is 'process conflict,' which is when disagreements arise on how the team should work together. Teams can minimize process conflict by agreeing how the team shares information, makes decisions, organizes meetings and other team work processes.

To address the question "How will we work together?" teams often create a team charter and a virtual team etiquette.

Team Charter

The team charter is the document that contains the agreements on how the team will work together. I often think that the process of creating the charter is actually more important than the charter itself, specifically the conversations that unearth the different assumptions various team members have about how to work together. Also, the agreement process sets a positive precedent for future cooperation. It is the first example of how the team can listen, share and work effectively together.

The team charter may include:

- Team Structure
    - Purpose
    - Scope
    - Time Commitment
    - Supporting Resources
    - Roles and Responsibilities
- Team Processes
    - Decision-Making Process
    - Communication Plan
    - External Stakeholder Management Plan
    - Team Rhythm: How Often the Team Meets
    - Expectations on Participation in the Team
    - Conflict Resolution Process
    - Feedback Process
    - Time Management Expectations
    - Information Sharing Processes
    - Communication Tools Use (see Task-Technology Fit)

Many of the items listed above may be expressed differently depending on the culture that one is from. Through conversations about these topics, and through working together and reviewing agreements, the team can uncover assumptions and converge on what is best for the team.

Virtual Team Etiquette

The virtual team etiquette is a document that provides guidelines for how the team use communication devices. The purpose of the document is to create an agreement so that working together is efficient and enjoyable for the team members. For instance, the team may have a rule that team members should not participate in meetings from their cars. The ambient noise is distracting and uncomfortable for the other members. Here are some other topics that may be included in the virtual team etiquette:

- **Rules on email use.** Whom to include in correspondence and whom to cc, expectation of response time, how to indicate urgency, how to indicate 'for your information only.'
- **One person one device in meetings.** Co-located team members may sit in the same room, however they each have their own screen so that they are always visible in the video meeting.
- **Scheduling.** How to keep the calendar up-to-date and how to schedule meetings, how to indicate availability, what type of contact is allowable after office hours in the case of an emergency.
- **Agreement on how to onboard new team members.** How to introduce them to the team and share the team norms and practices.
- **Meeting practices.** Fixed or rotating chairperson, determining the necessity for meeting attendance, role sharing (i.e., note taker, timekeeper, agenda minder), check-in and check-out practices.

A Word of Caution: Be Prepared to Adjust

The team may want to regularly revisit the team charter and virtual team etiquette to check if they still make sense for all team members. As mentioned in Chapter Three, Section titled Outside the Team, the local cultural norms and practices where the team members are located my impact the team collaboration in unexpected ways. As the team works together, they will notice which team norms work well and which need to be adjusted.

Knowing Each Other

'Who are my colleagues and where are they from?' is a question on the minds of new members of the virtual team. It is a question that can be easily answered, with intention and activities. It is possible to know the other team members. I have included many ideas in the section titled Virtual Team Building Exercises, so I will not repeat them here.

One of the underlying themes in this book is to build the relationships between team members and develop cultural competence to collaborate. Helping the team members to know each other to be able to build the foundation for collaboration is an important part of this Leadership Lever.

Should the Team Meet?

Challenge: You are the team leader of a new virtual project team that will work together for one year. You have the budget for one team event when everyone can meet in the same location for two days. When is the best time for your team to physically meet? Is it:

    A. In the beginning, immediately after the team members are assigned to the project

B. A few months into the project

C. Never; save the money

Let's review the options:

A. In the beginning. The standard advice is option A, to meet as soon as possible so that team members can know each other and build trust. This is a reasonable point of view and many team members have explained the benefit of an immediate meetings. "It was good to know my colleagues right away so that when I read their emails, I already knew who they were."

B. A few months into the project. On the other hand, option B also has some merit. Teams can develop and build trust virtually before the physical meeting. Certain topics are easier to discuss face-to-face, especially if they are difficult. If the team has been working together for a few months, they start to accumulate some irritations and issues, which could be discussed and resolved during the physical meeting, particularly if they had built the foundations of trust and relationship already.

I often hear a version of "When we met, it made all the difference. The issue that had been open and annoying all of us was easily resolved when we spent one hour together in the room with a flip chart. The dinner the night before already put us in a good mood, we had a great team spirit and there was a willingness to listen and adapt."

C. Never; save the money. Face-to-face meetings are one tool in the team's collection of communication tools and plays a role in the general development of the team. There is general consensus that face-to-face meetings can accelerate the development of personal connection and help to resolve conflicts. If a team chooses not to meet, then they may miss these benefits and must invest extra efforts in the online team development.

Whenever your team decides to meet, I recommend that it is a joint team decision. Team members may have a preference based on personality, cultural preferences or other criteria. Schedule the face-to-face meeting at a time when the impact for your team can be greatest, and fill the agenda with topics that benefit from physical presence, such as resolving conflict, finalizing critical decisions or contemplating the future.

When Meeting in Person is the Answer

Sometimes meeting in person can unstick a team that is stuck. Gabriela, a clever Frenchwoman, explained how a week-long visit from her counterpart at a key supplier was the critical shift in a partnership with a company in South Africa.

"We had a partnership to offer a new product on the market, and the South African company was our supplier. The program had already existed one year and I was brought in to bring it to the next phase. Our team were located mainly in Germany and France, and there was not much travel between Europe and S. Africa. Contact between us and them was mainly between a few people at the management level, and then the rest of the local team were responsible for implementing.

"Unfortunately the trust was quite low and we were having trouble achieving our goals. The previous phase was not completed on time, and there was a lot of blame going around. This was a tough environment to come into. I had some virtual meetings and phone calls with the South African counterparts, but I wasn't getting much traction.

"Someone suggested that we organize weekly calls between me as Project Director with my counterpart in South Africa. Unfortunately these calls did not work. We were struggling to discuss more than the issues list.

"To improve the collaboration, our managers decided to send my counterpart in South Africa to Germany to visit us. She spent a week with *me and we went to dinner and exhibitions with other colleagues. And then we became friends. Now she writes to me regularly on WhatsApp. It turned into a nice relationship and this helped with the business relationship. She helped me to gain the trust of the other people in South Africa as she spoke highly of me. Soon after her visit, there was a shift in which communication improved and things started to flow."*

As this story highlights, spending time together can be the magic oil for collaboration. Consider different options for your team and use the travel budgets for the greatest impact.

Key Points

- Virtual team members face unknowns when they join a team, which could be known. For instance, who are the team members and how the team will work together? These are usually easier to know in co-located teams.
- Team leaders can actively help the team members to know these topics and thereby eliminate the uncertainty that the team members feel.
- Often team leaders immediately discuss the work and do not realize the importance of spending time on these topics which are unknown but could be known.

CHAPTER 6

Create the Team

Only 10% of leaders have the ability to 'anticipate and respond to rapidly changing conditions and to effectively manage complex, interdependent relationships.' This sobering statistic comes from William B. Joiner and Stephen A. Josephs in their book *Leadership Agility: Five Levels of Mastery for Anticipating and Initiating Change.*[1] The remaining 90% can be summarized into a phrase, *heroic leadership.*

Joiner and Josephs' research proves what we see in many organizations. Traditionally the organizational mantra was for strong, decisive, visionary leaders. We label this heroic leadership because the leader is in the center, and all employees turn their gaze towards him. An example is the traditional hub-and-spoke leadership style, in which the leader directs the actions of the team members, resolves issues with his expertise and maintains the information flow within and outside of the team. Another example is the achievement-oriented leader who sets the direction, manages resources and key stakeholders and focuses on reaching the objectives. In both of these teams, the leader is necessary to complete the work.

Unfortunately the leader with the heroic style of leadership will struggle to lead his global virtual teams. He simply cannot be everywhere, all the time. He will want to know everything that is happening with the team members, he will want to ensure everyone is working on his directives, and he will want to manage all the stakeholders effectively. And he will be frustrated and may long for the overview and control he had when working with his co-located team.

One of the greatest limitations of the heroic leadership style is the almost noose-like strangle on the team potential in the dynamic, quickly changing business world. When all decisions and directions are by the team leader, then speed slows down and the range of information is confined. Global virtual teams need a different type of leadership that leverages the broad capacity and information of the team and fosters an agile team culture for the accelerating change.

Many thought leaders have identified post-heroic leadership as the more effective leadership style for the current dynamic business environment. Joiner and Josephs call this Catalyst Leadership and define it (from their book):

View of Leadership: Visionary, facilitative orientation. Believes that leaders articulate an innovative, inspiring vision and bring together the right people to transform the vision into reality. Leaders empower others and actively facilitate their development.

Agility in Pivotal Conversations: Adept at balancing assertive and accommodative styles as needed in particular situations. Likely to articulate and question underlying assumptions. Genuinely interested in learning from diverse viewpoints. Proactive in seeking and applying feedback.

Agility in Leading Teams: Intent on creating a highly participative team. Acts as a team leader and facilitator. Provides and seeks open exchange of views on difficult issues. Empowers direct reports. Uses team development as a vehicle for leadership development.

106

These words point to a leadership mindset focused on the team, its development and deep understanding of the different perspectives of everyone involved. This leadership style is appropriate for a global virtual team. The gap created by the physical absence of the team leader is filled with an agile and collaborative team. The focus of the team leader is to facilitate the creation of that team.

Types of Virtual Teams

In my consulting practice, many clients want support to help teams in their organizations improve the collaboration across different locations. When we review the CALDO model together, they notice cultural diversity and immediately attribute cultural differences as the source of the problem. However, when I interview the team members and diagnose the situation, I discover that one of the Levers of the CALDO model has not been give enough attention. The team have not identified the correct team type and then under the Lever Create the Team, built the appropriate team.

They have misdiagnosed their team type because the geographic distance causes people to feel and think more separated than they actually need to be to achieve their goals. They tend to be more transactional with each other and much less supportive.

The following scenario is a version of situations I often encounter. Within the same company, a factory in Norway sends product to the distribution and sales office in the US, who deliver to the final customer. To begin, the functional differences give a sense of separation, and then the geographic distance and cultural diversity add to the feeling. The colleagues behave in the following ways:

- **Very transactional.** They expect orders and deliveries to be as per the service agreement documentation.
- **Viewing from their own perspective.** They interpret behaviors and assume business based on their own local conditions. They may often say, 'Why do they need that?' or 'That does not make sense' when they hear what the other location requests.
- **Blame the other location.** Neutral people assessing the tension see both sides of the story, but the people in each location do not.

If the customers' orders were standard and the factory produced commodities, then the transactional relationship would probably be adequate and a service agreement could be applied in most of the cases. However, the clients who contact me have customized products, demanding customers and quickly changing markets. A transactional collaboration is wholly inadequate and they need a productive, collaborative 'we are in this together' team mindset.

When teams identify their team type accurately, they realize the necessity of creating a team that matches the amount of necessary collaboration to achieve their goals.

Virtual Team Type

Virtual teams can be classified into four team types based on the level of task interdependence, meaning how much colleagues need to interact to complete the work. These classifications were defined by Professors Bell and Kozlowski, who at the time of the article were both at Michigan State University.[2] (Figure 6.1)

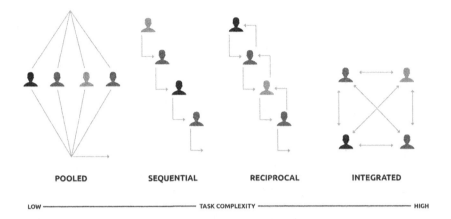

| POOLED | SEQUENTIAL | RECIPROCAL | INTEGRATED |

LOW ——————————————————— TASK COMPLEXITY ——————————————————— HIGH

Figure 6.1 Type of Virtual Teams, Bell and Kozlowski. The lines indicate communication pathways between colleagues at different locations.

Pooled: Pooled teams agree in the beginning on what each team member needs to deliver. Everyone works independently and delivers the agreed output with little interaction in between. They agree what needs to be done, but how each person works on their deliverable is independent and not of consequence to the rest of the team.

Example: A team of consultants each work at a different site of a client to implement a common solution. They only connect once a week to discuss the progress on each site. Each consultant works on his assignment and handles the client location on his own.

Sequential: Colleague A independently completes a task and passes the output to Colleague B, who independently completes a task and passes the output to Colleague C.

Example: A local shipping department sends monthly figures to their local finance department, who then create financial reports that are sent to the regional finance department, who in turn compile the results for the countries in the region and send the results to headquarters. Everyone is dependent on someone else to provide data, but their calculation process, the contact with stakeholders and the approval process are independent of the colleagues from whom and to whom they send the information.

Reciprocal: Reciprocal teams are active with coordination and exchange of information. The exchange of information is ongoing, and Colleagues A and B have a back-and-forth exchange until Colleague B completes the work and sends it onto another colleague. These teams may produce non-standard work, which requires an iterative question-and-answer exchange.

Example: A team that consists of different functions assigned and completed in different locations. The team need to discuss and align on what they will do together and also how they will work together. They will agree on coordination, communication channels, stakeholder management and process integration. By understanding what their colleagues will do with the information or product they send, they can better prepare their work. For instance, if manufacturing, marketing and sales are in three different locations, they will coordinate with each other, align on deliverables and send information back and forth to support each other. However, they do not need to agree as to how each function will do the work.

Integrated: These are virtual teams in which the work between the team members is coordinated from different locations. They create, research, experiment, organize, decide, reject and undertake all other team processes within the team. These teams converge on what they will do and how they will work together.

Example: A 100% virtual software team who create new solutions together. They work intensely together and are continuously checking that everyone is aligned.

In the example I gave at the beginning of this section, the Norway-US team thought of themselves as sequential, when they needed to act as reciprocal. They thought a service agreement would be enough, but they needed a relationship based on trust, shared objectives and culturally competent team members, willing to think beyond their own local markets.

Identify the Team Type to Create the Team

The team leader of a pooled team will need to spend less time and energy to create a team than to a team leader of an integrated team, who needs to ensure everyone knows each other, the purpose and objectives are clear and how the team will work together has been agreed upon and is regularly reviewed and updated.[3]

Returning to the Norway-US team, in spite of all the signals of separation, they need to strengthen their working relationships. Returning to the CALDO model, they need to recognize the impact of distance and cultural diversity on their collaboration, focus on the 4 Leadership Levers, monitor the attitudes such as trust and psychological safety and develop the competences of the team members. They had planned that a service-level agreement could replace the need to intentionally develop working relationships, but the resulting issues prove that more intense relationships are needed.

Although the example I referenced involved a manufacturing company, I often find this issue arising in IT companies where the software development is in one country and the client interface in another country or in shared service center constructions. The people involved feel separated when they need to think, feel and act connected.

Shared Purpose and Goals

Peter did everything right on his virtual team of Quality Control Managers, who were located in different countries of North and South America. "We had team building exercises virtually, and they worked," he began. "They were fun and people got to know each other. Everything went well for the first year, but now we seem to have lost our energy and I am not sure what to do." As Peter and I discussed his team, we realized what was missing, which was that the team had lost their shared goals and purpose. In the first year, they had common KPIs and a shared purpose to impact the quality conditions in the Americas organization. But due to a reorganization, the current vague purpose was to share knowledge. It was not compelling enough to keep all the very busy team members engaged. Peter noticed a difference. "If I had this situation when I worked with my team in my factory, I could speak individually with them and keep them motivated. With the virtual team so far away, my one-on-one discussions just don't seem to move the needle as much." Teams need common elements that will bind them together cognitively, emotionally and behaviorally.

Team Purpose

Many team leaders I speak with say something along the lines of "The team has team annual targets. That should be enough." From a cognitive viewpoint, it is enough; however, most team members want to be engaged emotionally as well. They want to feel proud to be part of a team.

The team purpose is the reason why the team exists and can be the guiding light for the team. By articulating the team purpose, the team members become more conscious of the role they have both within and beyond their team.

Global virtual teams often have a broader purpose because they have a regional or even global impact. This could be a point to emphasize to help the team members to appreciate their purpose as a team.

Benefit and Challenge to Common Goals

Most team leaders I speak with confirm that their team have clear common goals that are measurable, documented and 'should be known by everyone.' Team members can be motivated by common goals for a few reasons. To begin, if they see other team members working toward a goal that is important to them, they will feel motivated to contribute. Further, often people are motivated if they believe that their contribution will make a difference in something bigger than themselves, and they see others doing the same.

Global virtual teams often have conflicting goals and objectives, which can hinder the motivational impact of shared goals. Global teams are often embedded in matrix organizations where team members have multiple objectives and measurements, often in conflict with each other. Team members then need to navigate the dilemmas and consider different ways to manage the areas of tension.

Shared goals are motivating. Conflicting goals are frustrating at best and trust-draining at worst. When teams have open conversations about the conflicting goals, they can map out the tensions and devise solutions.

Team Spirit with Symbols

What type of animal is your team? Teams often enjoy and benefit from exercises that find metaphors or symbols to portray the team. Virtual teams benefit from a strong *esprit de corps* and a positive energy that unites the team. It is particularly valuable during difficult stages of the project.

Team symbols can be especially engaging for virtual team members because they act as a reminder of their team. A coffee mug with a picture of the team from the last on-site event or a mouse pad with a screen-shot of everyone's face during a video call is an example.

Matthew, a virtual team leader, proudly told me how his regional team created their team name. "We created a team name together; everyone submitted a team name and we all agreed on Marketing R Us. This created a shared sense of identity, which I think is important."

Symbols are only effective if they represent a true team spirit and not a team that does not connect with each other. Team leaders need to continuously give oxygen to team spirit by reminding the team why they are together, encouraging the team to connect with each other, and celebrate the successes of the team. Remember, the distance can quickly cause the team spirit to diminish, and team leaders need to support the team to feel connected.

Maintaining the Team

The shared purpose, goals and norms are just the start to grab the attention and enthusiasm of the team members. As mentioned in the section on Shared Team Identity, global virtual teams benefit from having a positive and intentional team identity. I use the word *intentional* because often, team identities are difficult to create from a distance. If left to chance, most likely the local identities will dominate any weak virtual team identity.

With that in mind, below are some ideas to maintain the feeling of a team.[4]

Positive team feedback. The leader reminds the team what they have accomplished together and how their collaboration made a difference. She continuously praises the team publicly, such as in a chat room or an email, and shares feedback from other stakeholders as well.

Common goals and contributions. The leader will incorporate the shared purpose and impact for a 'we're all in this together and we need each of you' mentality. He will mention these shared elements regularly in meetings, documents and informal communication. Team members feel connected to the team because they understand their own contribution and that of others.

Team activities. The team leader points to successful activities that the team recently accomplished to remind team members of their shared connection. For instance, she would say "At the last meeting when we created the strategy together" or "Remember the virtual team building exercise we did in February that we all enjoyed and learned?" Through these recollections, the team members feel a shared experience.

Support to the individual. The team leader focuses on each individual's needs, and by doing so, each person feels emotionally part of the team. For instance, the team leader actively draws out each person's feedback during meetings, encourages and values different opinions and creates a nurturing experience for everyone. The team leader acts as a supportive coach, serves each person's individual needs and gives the feeling of availability so that the team members do not feel alone. Finally, he ensures everyone has the same information and access to his support.

Many virtual teams have successfully created a connected team who support and collaborate from various locations. A major ingredient of the connection is that they feel to be part of the same team.

Knowledge Sharing

I meet many virtual team leaders who dream of a team who seamlessly share knowledge across locations. They see the potential breakthroughs if colleagues would just talk. As one manager explained, "Often I have to be the coordinator and remind them of each other's existence. I say 'go speak with Jim as he has experience in that topic', but they hesitate, and ignore my suggestion."

The paradox is that virtual teams have more diverse information to share compared to co-located teams, but they have the tendency to share less. In hybrid teams, colleagues experience *co-located blindness*, which means they seek the opinions of co-located colleagues even if contacting the virtual colleague would lead to a better result.[5] This can be a wasted opportunity, particularly in teams who are innovating or addressing critical business challenges. As has been noted in research:

Previous research has consistently found that informationally diverse teams are more effective in performing tasks that are uncertain, complex, non-routine, and interdependent.[6]

Team Memory System

The words *Transactive Memory System* may sound so academic that many of you will probably want to close the book right now. But before you do, let's focus on one of the words, memory. The definition of memory is 'the faculty by which the mind stores and remembers information' (Oxford Dictionary).

Can a team have a memory? According to the Transactive Memory System concept, the answer is yes. A team memory can also serve the team in the same way that our own memories serve us in the storage and retrieval of information. I think of the team memory system as a network of lights, whereby each light represents a person. The lights blink every time information is retrieved from a team member. The more the team memory system is activated, the more the flickering.

To improve knowledge sharing within the team, a team leader may want to consciously create a team memory system. To create the conditions for knowledge sharing, I would like to reference the CALDO model to identify the key elements in a holistic approach:

Levers

Create the team. The starting point is the creation of the team with clear shared purpose and goals. The team members understand the role of each person and their own contribution to the team. When they know the other also identifies with the team, they feel they are in this together and are more likely to share with each other.

Team Members

Who Knows What. In a new team, no one is sure what the others know. The team would benefit from activities and conversations that identify where certain expertise is located. For instance, an exercise starting with the question 'You can come to me for…', in which each team member offers their help, opens the door for an interaction. Also, the team can celebrate if someone has completed a training program or if a team member has applied their expertise in a new and innovative way.

Cultural Diversity

Develop Cultural Competence. Team members may perceive the different country contexts and communication styles as hurdles for the knowledge sharing process. As team members develop cultural competence, they will have the capacity to interact with colleagues from other countries and share knowledge in more meaningful ways.

Attitude

Trust and Psychological Safety.[7] Team members request guidance and offer advice and expertise when they feel that the relationship is surrounded with trust and psychological safety. The requester will initiate the conversation when he knows the other will welcome the initiative. The knowledge expert will share information when she knows that her expertise is respected and her advice will not be misused.

Levers

Adapt with the Times. Just like your own memory is continuously chang-ing, so is that of a team, especially one in a dynamic environment. Teams with effective memory systems do two things. Firstly, team members will share new information that they come across with the experts on the team to support them and help them to stay up to date. For instance, an account manager hears of a new technical development at a competitor and informs the product engineer. Secondly, the experts continuously share updates with the team so that they know when to contact them for advice. This reiterative process helps the experts to stay fresh and the team to know who knows what.

Encourage Connections. Encourage, reward and highlight regularly when team members turn to each other for help and information. Try to make this a team norm. The team should understand the impact of a well-developed team memory system and how they can contribute to its maintenance.

Team leaders can create the environment for knowledge sharing by recognizing how distance and cultural diversity cause team members to be reluctant to contact each other. The leader can intentionally take actions to encourage, support and reward the creation of a team memory system with the blinking lights of an active network.

Virtual Team Building Exercises

It is ironical that virtual teams need more but often have less interaction than co-located teams. Team building exercises can fill the gap and are probably easier to schedule than meeting together in person.

Team building exercises come in many shapes and sizes, and I would like to look at two types, namely, team bonding and online games. Team bonding exercises are activities in which participants reveal something about themselves through questions, drawings, objects or other triggers. Online games are fun to play when participants compete or work together toward a shared goal, which is not directly related to work. Researchers at University of Saskatchewan found online games can be more effective for trust building than social icebreakers.[8] They reasoned that online games create an environment for risk taking and interdependence, and team members experiment with each other through play. In the end, online games, team bonding exercises and social icebreakers complement each other and would be valuable to include during the early stages of team formation.

Types of Team Building

When the team is first forming and members need to bond with each other, one-hour activities that focus on the team members can help build trust and connection. Generally, these conversations should combine professional and personal topics, and be inviting so that people feel safe to speak. Here are some ideas:

- **Tell your story.** Everyone draws a picture that tells something about themselves. The drawing is not a timeline, per se, but a few key items that show important moments or relationships. Each person takes a photo, shares it with the other colleagues and tells their story.
- **Virtual office tour.** Most team members are curious where their colleagues are located. Use the computer or mobile phone to guide the colleagues on an office tour to give each other a feel of the surroundings.
- **Personality assessment.** Teams may benefit from personality

assessments, which can trigger insightful conversations about working styles and preferences. For instance, teams may use Structural Dynamics, Belbin Team Roles, Management Drives or Strengths Finder, often facilitated by an expert.

- **Professional success.** Ask a question that highlights a positive work experience for each person. For instance, 'Tell us a high-energy experience in your professional life' or 'When did you really enjoy your work?'
- **Attend an online course together.** When teams learn together they can participate in a shared experience and also apply the learnings to the team context. The topic can be work related or something more inspirational, such as art history.

Social icebreakers at the beginning of a meeting are a quick way to maintain the personal connection in a team. Some teams prefer light questions such as 'What do you see out your window?' whereas other teams prefer more work-oriented topics such as 'What is the latest news at your factory site?' Teams often alternate the questions to keep team members interested. These questions only require a few minutes for everyone to answer and can be a worthwhile team ritual to sustain the team spirit. Here are a few ideas:

- What was your first job?
- What is your favorite movie?
- What is on your bucket list, personally and professionally?
- What industry book or article have you recently read?
- What is your favorite public holiday in your country?
- Whom do you admire and why?
- Which of the company values speaks to you the most and why?

Time for team building is a worthwhile investment for a virtual team. The exercises bring informality and humanity to a very technology-oriented relationship. Teams may choose from a plethora of exercises and must make the time and effort to reap the benefits.

Key Points

- As the team leader cannot be everywhere, all the time, a collaborative team fills the gap. Virtual team leaders should strengthen the connections between the team members and support their development.
- By identifying the virtual team type, a team leader can determine which information the team members need to know about how other colleagues work and what they are doing.
- Teams often consider themselves to be less interdependent then they need to be given the complexity of their situation. Geographic distance and cultural diversity may give a feeling of separation when the teams need to feel close.
- An advantage of multi-location teams is knowledge sharing. However, virtual teams need trust and psychological safety to create a team environment where the benefits can be realized.
- Although teams are not physically together, they can enjoy team-building exercises that build trust and relationships.

CHAPTER 7

Bring in the Humanity

This entire book is about connecting humans. But as we type into a computer, put on a headphone, send a message to an email address and add comments to a shared document, we may lose the human touch that makes us and the others feel real. The third Leadership Lever, Bring in the Humanity, puts a spotlight on the extra attention that can make a difference as to how people feel and engage on a virtual team.

This chapter contains concepts and examples that can help team leaders to actively care for and support the people in their virtual teams. The chapter begins with how leaders can show personal attention for the colleagues, even from a distance. The chapter also includes topics that are similar to those for a co-located team, but without physical presence, the necessity to be explicit with these topics heightens. For instance, co-located team members may perceive a leader as fair because they share the same cultural assumptions and can see the leader's expressions. For them, the fairness of the decisions is obvious. This may not be the case in a virtual team, and the multicultural team benefit when the leader is more explicit about the decision process. This is the extra effort that recognizes the humans on the team and their needs to feel part of the team.

As you progress through the chapter, you may notice that these ideas are easily within reach for the virtual leader who wants to bring out the best in his or her virtual team.

Personal Attention from a Distance

The irony of virtual leadership is that distant team members may need more personal attention than local team members, but giving personal attention from a distance may seem intimidating or unnatural. Distant team members need more personal attention because they may feel isolated and cautious of the support they can ask of others. They are often uncertain about their career chances, since they may have little contact with key decision makers. Like everyone, they experience the ups and downs of life and may not receive the consideration in their workload. Colleagues cannot see what is happening to them.

On the other hand, the team leader can easily see the sullen faces of the local colleagues who are struggling, or notice the extra hours invested by the driven colleague. But these techniques fall flat in a virtual setting.

The personal attention of a leader often has an indirect impact on results, through the engagement, motivation and satisfaction of the team members. In this section, I consider three types of personal attention. They are care and empathy, developmental support and appreciation.

Care and Empathy

"Leadership is not about being in charge. Leadership is about taking care of those in your charge." These words, from Simon Sinek in his popular video on Understanding Empathy, emphasize a crucial aspect of leadership, irrespective of location. Great virtual leaders can care for their colleagues even from a distance.

Listen for Changes
"I listen to how they speak during a meeting. If I hear them speaking faster than usual, or sounding more distant, then I follow-up with a

phone call because that could mean that they are over stressed or some-thing else. Also, if they take longer than usual to answer an email, then I follow-up. You get a feeling when you work with people very closely, even virtually, you know their working style, so you can capture things if something is out of the ordinary. I try to notice changes in their usual behavior or working pattern because that could be a sign that something is wrong." These words are from Jennie, a leader of a virtual team in three countries. Jennie used all of her senses to pay attention to the status of her colleague. But she did not just listen, she took action with a follow-up phone call or video chat.

Consider Their Situation

Caring from a distance means that you are thinking of the other per-son, making sure they are well and doing what you can to help. For instance, we heard from one of Goran's employees in India how he showed that he cared. "Due to the workload, there were times when we would flex our hours and start late and end late. Goran arranged with our local manager so that we had taxis to go home. He understood that taking public transportation in the dark was more dangerous. He really thought about us."

To consider the situation of someone else in a different location means that the leader appreciates the culture and other dynamics there. A good place to begin is with curiosity and genuine interest in the welfare of others.

> *Monica is the Operational Director and the leader of a 100%*
> *remote team. She exemplifies a caring virtual leader and shared a*
> *story. "At the beginning of every team call, we go around and share*
> *with each other how we are, what is our focus for the week, and what*
> *is getting our attention this week. When David did his sharing, he said*

125

'I am in Vietnam.' So my ears prick up, why is he not in Singapore, where he lives. He said, 'We are just waiting for my wife's visa to come through.' I thought, ok, but he seemed quiet on the call. We went through the call and through our agenda. After the call, I messaged David, 'Hey, it would be good to catch up.' I found out that he had problems with his wife's visa to go back to Singapore. He needed financial data for the last three years to support his application. I offered our support and quickly arranged for the financial director to gather the data for him. With that information, he could complete the application. That is an example of the extra care when people may be experiencing a difficult time. We want to support people not just with their work life, but also as human beings, since we bring our whole selves when we turn on the screen. We are showing up as a whole person. That is where I would follow-up and see what is happening. You just notice something is not right."

Create the Communication Pathways

A well-established communication pathway has the same impact as seeing a well-worn path in a forest. It is inviting, low-risk and leads to somewhere desirable. Team members will use communication pathways to easily reach out to colleagues and team leaders for work issues, but also for personal reasons. Team leaders can establish communication pathways by taking initiative, using the different communication tools and communicating regularly.

Respond Timely and Make Time

Team members feel that they are supported when they receive answers to their questions or problems in a timely manner. This does not mean that you need to provide immediate answers every time your phone beeps.

It does mean that you agree on a way for team members to contact you when they require special attention, and that you respond accordingly.

Along these same lines, leaders can respond to informal requests for time. "Do you have a moment?" is an important question from a distant colleague and should be received with a "Yes" as often as possible.

Send Notes or Gifts

Although you may not be able to be present with a kind look or a pat on the shoulder, you can still show that you are thinking of your colleague when they have a difficult time or a celebration. Flowers, cards and other gifts can be symbols of caring, as long as you consider the cultural context.

Developmental Support

One-on-One

During the interviews and informal conversations I had while researching this book, I heard team members value the one-on-one sessions they have with their managers. The generic structure is a regular meeting (usually biweekly or monthly) between the manager and team member, and the agenda is set by the team member. They could discuss anything that was not directly related to tasks, such as career development, work-life balance issues and conflict resolutions with colleagues. Virtual team members can feel isolated, so these sessions may help them feel heard and supported by someone who can make a difference.

Patrick, a manager in England, explained the additional advantage of the one-on-one meetings with his team in India. "The one-on-one meetings were very important because I wanted the team in India to contact me anytime there was a problem. But they wouldn't do so if they did not feel they had access to me. The one-on-one sessions helped us to get to know each other and that I am available for them."

Dorene, a manager in Texas, experienced a surprising development in her hybrid virtual team because of the virtual one-on-one meetings. "In the beginning I only used them for the remote team members as this was their moment to have access to me, which the local colleagues always had. But we realized the locals had me sporadically, and they were missing a regular scheduled moment for themselves. So we set up regular one-on-one meetings with the local team members as well."

Build the Network to Show You Care

In the classic matrix organization, most employees have a direct reporting line to a manager, and indirect reporting line(s) to other managers for projects or other strategic reasons. The virtual employee benefits when the direct and indirect managers align on the shared interests of the employee.

This was the issue when I consulted for a multinational with a matrix organization. The virtual team members were struggling between the direct and indirect managers, sometimes resulting in legal issues because of various country laws and practices. When the direct and indirect managers connected on their shared interest, the welfare of the employee, they were able to find workable solutions.

Attention to Career Development

When the managers are in another location, team members wonder if they will have the same exposure to high-profile positions, or if they will have influential people advocating for them during promotion conversations. The motto 'out of site, out of mind' can cause an issue for career growth and development.

Team leaders can address these concerns by having regular

conversations with each team member about their career development and the various options they could consider. The managers can help the team members to navigate the organization. For instance, participation in high-profile projects, introduction to key decision makers or additional education to gain credibility.

During the interviews, I spoke with virtual team leaders and with people on their team. One key theme was that the virtual team leaders did not let the distance prevent them from supporting and helping their team members to develop. And the team members acknowledged and valued this effort by the team leader, such as advice, coaching, mentoring and other support when necessary.

Showing Appreciation

Most employees are motivated by recognition and appreciation for the work or extra efforts they have done, and this includes distant colleagues as well. Since they miss the informal interaction with co-located colleagues, they may require more frequent messages to hear they are valued. As with all communication, consider the cultural context as well. An American 'Excellent job!' may be considered over the top or embarrassing in China.

Tell Them

Using video conferencing to show his sincerity, a team leader can inform the colleagues why he values them. Teams can benefit from a bonding exercise in which everyone tells each other what they value about each other. If you do this virtually, you can use breakout rooms to organize the one-on-one sessions.

Colleagues Show Appreciation

In high performing teams, team members will also show appreciation to their colleagues who put in extra effort on a project, who shared their knowledge or who helped to make valuable local connections.

Intellectual Stimulation

Imagine you are working and your manager walks by your desk and asks for a few minutes of your time. She sits down and starts probing a problem and wants your input. You are glad she asks you to think along, and you contribute new ideas that she had not considered. You are surprised by some things she says, which make you rethink what you knew. After 20 minutes, she leaves and you return to your work, glad to have been part of that conversation.

Most people who work virtually are knowledge workers who want the experience of intellectual stimulation to remain motivated and engaged.[1] It helps them to improve their current knowledge and contribute to the team. An advantage of virtual working is the potential for more intellectual stimulation than in a co-located team. The breadth of geographic reach means that there is more to know, but only if that potential is conscientiously tapped. The default is to focus on tasks and agendas.

This is another moment when an intentional leader can help the virtual team to go beyond the distance issues and help to realize the potential of the team. Teams who feel connected and have norms and practices to inquire, evaluate and question the *status quo* can be more creative. For instance, create a practice in which team members supply new information to regular meetings or to the team chat site with the intention of questioning a current practice.

Many of us enjoy the buzz that comes when our mind is turned on. In the busy meeting-filled days, leaders sometimes miss how important this is for team members. Putting attention on this topic yourself, or nominating a team member to take on the role of intellectual stimulator, can help your team to be more creative and engaged.

Recovery

One physical rule for top athletes is that muscles break down during the sport, and build while resting. Building endurance and power is a combination of intense training and recovery.

This combination is also true for knowledge workers who work globally. They are satisfied to work internationally and like the learning potential *if* they have time for off-job recovery.

Professors Nurmi and Hinds, of Aalto University and Stanford University, respectively, interviewed and surveyed knowledge workers and found that they enjoy many characteristics of global work.[2] This may be surprising, since several aspects such as time zones, technology and lack of human contact are considered onerous by my virtual workers. And yet, the researchers identified two categories of advantages that knowledge workers would miss if they only worked locally.

The first category was the job complexity of global work. Knowledge workers valued that they were in a position to develop their communication, coordination and innovation skills. They also enjoyed the higher autonomy that often accompanies virtual work and the chance to develop themselves to take more ownership of their own work. Additionally, since global projects or work tends to have more impact on the company than local projects, many knowledge workers experience more meaning in their contribution.

The second category was the greater learning opportunity offered by working globally and virtually. When people work with colleagues from other cultures and backgrounds, they have the possibility to learn new ways of working, advanced technology or a unique view of life. Knowledge workers put learning high on their value list, and global work can fill that need.

However, global work takes energy. Time zone differences may result in early or late hours. Listening, speaking, writing and reading in a second language all day can be exhausting. Staying on top of the progress of colleagues requires attention.

The researchers found that to work at this top level and experience the satisfaction of job complexity and learning opportunities, global workers needed to check out, turn off and mentally and physically recover in their own way. People who did not have time to recover did not consider their work beneficial, even if job complexity was high and learning opportunities were offered. They were simply too tired to enjoy them.

Global working invites us to be present 24/7, but we need to decline the invitation.

Companies are realizing the risk of exhausted global employees and are implementing policies to give them time for recovery. For instance, some policies state that employees cannot send emails after work hours or on weekends. Other companies encourage employees to go home at normal work hours, turn off the tools and technically check out.

Team leaders, just like sport coaches, can create a team culture with practices that respect off-job recovery time. Each team should discuss and agree how the team members will respect the recovery time of each other so that the team can work at high performance together.

Giving Feedback

Virtual managers frequently ask for advice on giving feedback. They consider talent development a critical element of their role, and they want the feedback to be meaningful. But they are unsure of how to approach the feedback conversation when the feedback receiver is not in the same room.

Many companies support their managers with feedback scripts and steps to make the feedback process easier and more effective for everyone. *Give feedback within a reasonable time. Give concrete examples. End on a positive note and with an action plan for improvement.* This is a good start but needs additional attention because giving feedback to a virtual team member may be somewhat challenging for a number of reasons.

- The receiver is from another culture and therefore has different expectations and communication practices. The words of the feedback giver may be heard in a different way than what was intended.
- As mentioned in Chapter Three, section titled Between the Locations, the distance causes people to view the remote colleagues as abstract. The feedback giver will need to reference specific details that are meaningful for the receiver.
- The manager only has a vague idea of the daily experience of the feedback receiver. The employee does her work, but how she spends her day is difficult to imagine. She interacts with colleagues, engages in customer relationship management and handles local issues. The manager will likely not understand the entire context within which she operates.
- The feedback exchange is through communication technology. Once the receiver leaves the virtual office (i.e., turns off the video or hangs up the phone), then the manager has no idea how the

feedback receiver reacts or feels. This may be unsettling for the manager, who wants to care for the employee as she processes the feedback.

With this in mind, the feedback guidelines need to be expanded for the virtual leader and include the following:[3]

- Before you give the feedback, check with a trusted colleague who may know the cultural context of your feedback receiver. Perhaps they can give you insights and clarity to your understanding of the situation.
- Approach the conversation as if you are missing some of the information and do not know the entire story. Then you would be more inclined to inquire, listen and alter your opinion.
- Be prepared to explain your point of view more than you would when speaking with someone nearby. Your opinion may be influenced by the norms and practices of your location, which may be unknown to your virtual colleague.
- Use the richest technology available, such as video meeting or phone, and follow up with the colleague during the days thereafter. Most people process feedback in their own way, such as internal reflections or conversations with confidants, and may want to add more to the feedback conversation with you.

With care and attention, the virtual leader can support the team member's development and learning through their international experience.

Fairness

Most managers have faced issues of fairness sometime in their teams. It may have been about workload, pay raise, career advancement or task allocation. Team members who perceive that they have not been treated fairly may mentally resign or check out, or perhaps even worse, they may spend time complaining about how they have been treated. Most managers will try to show and explain how they have been fair to calm the waters.

In virtual teams, the perception of fairness is even more necessary because the colleagues do not have the physical cues to help them understand the reasons for the decisions.[4] Imagine the following scenario: You are a manager who is located in China with a team consisting of people in three locations-China, Vietnam and UAE. You decide to divide the tasks amongst the team and give the more interesting work to the colleagues in China, and the boring tasks to your colleagues in Vietnam. For the team members in UAE, you give the work that requires interaction with stakeholders across other time zones, which may require longer working hours.

The people in Vietnam and UAE find this unfair, not because you made the decision, but because you seemed to do so without considering their situations and how the decision would impact their career aspirations and their work-life balance. They are disappointed and less engaged, feeling sidelined due to the beneficial treatment to your local colleagues. You wonder why the team seems withdrawn in the following meetings and why they seem disengaged from their work.

Now imagine another scenario. You ask for input from everyone about the allocation of tasks. You make the same decision, but you understand the impact of your decision on the team members in the different locations and you explain your reasoning for the decision. Specifically, you want the Chinese team to do the more interesting work because they have recently taken a course on the technique and you want them to first verify and then teach the technique to the colleagues in Vietnam and UAE. You also explain that the local HR support in UAE has allowed the team to flex their hours to accommodate the time zone challenges.

So you make the same decision, but you have considered the local impact and have explained the decision in a way that the team members feel that they have been heard. You explain the short-term decision with the long-term vision, and everyone has a chance for input. All team members find this to be fair and are engaged and enthusiastic about the project.

The difference can be summarized in two actions that contribute to a climate of fairness in decision-making: Consideration of the different contexts and communication in a transparent way to be understood.

As team leaders make decisions that impact the team, an environment of fairness can increase team members' engagement and motivation.

Perceived Proximity

People Will Feel Closer Than They Appear

Even though colleagues might be far away from each other, they can still feel close. This is called *perceived closeness* and can impact the quality of the working relationship.

"I meet John (my co-located colleague) every day but we don't have time to talk daily, but I talk with Ben (my distant colleague) almost every day. Ben feels closer even though he's miles away from me." This quote, and the others in this section, is from a participant in a study by Professors O'Leary, Wilson and Metiu of Georgetown University, College of William and Mary and ESSEC Business School, respectively.[5] They surveyed almost

700 international respondents and found that perceived proximity, and not actual physical proximity, impacted relationship quality. They also found that perceived closeness is created through communication and shared identity.

When team members communicate, they give impressions of dependability, reliability and personal characteristics such as kindness, intelligence and humor. Particularly in the beginning, when the question 'Who is my colleague?' hangs in the air, frequent communication can start to provide answers. Even if the communication is about work, personal characteristics will start to seep through. Often, the more people speak together, the deeper and more human their conversations become. The type of communication may vary, but as mentioned in the section titled Technology, rich communication tools can help to send more cues in the beginning of a relationship.

The other component that helps colleagues to feel closer to each other is a shared identity, meaning that they identify with each other. The shared identity may be a social identity, such as the fact that they are both mothers. Or it may be a team identity, since they are both on the same project. Shared identity may show up in many different ways. For instance, two people who are equally committed to the work may feel a closeness to each other. Similar training, professional background, attitudes, skills, personal values or demographics. When colleagues feel a common identity, they start to feel closer.

The reason identity decreases psychological distance is that colleagues can imagine what the other person is like or how they live, even without detailed information. If I know my distant colleague is also writing a book, then I can imagine some of the struggles he also faces and fill in the picture of who he is as a person. It helps us to relate, connect and feel closer.

Interestingly, shared identity is usually found through communication.

137

So we are back to communication, which is an opportunity to create meaningful connection with each other. Over time, the communication often becomes deeper in substance and understanding.

As perceived closeness requires commitment, time and energy, colleagues may want to be intentional with whom they create the closeness. Generally, the more complex the work, the greater the need for perceived closeness. Colleagues need to feel that they know the other well enough to collaborate. For instance, in the section titled Types of Virtual Teams, the reciprocal and integrated teams would benefit from team members feeling close to each other.

Sometimes I hear virtual teams say, "When we met, it did not matter. We were already feeling close to each other." Colleagues who feel close to each other are more likely to help each other, share information, learn together, put in the extra effort and commit to the team. Closeness in spite of the geographic distance is both possible and highly beneficial for a global virtual team.

The Feeling of Closeness

Kiogi is a team leader in Brazil and is responsible for a team located in India. The team's two-year project was to centralize all the IT support in one location. Kiogi was born and raised in Brazil by parents who were originally from Japan. Through his multicultural background, he had a high degree of cultural competence.

I was curious to hear about the experience of his team and was glad to interview Kiogi and his team members in India. Ayann described Kiogi as a leader who encouraged them to take ownership but at the same time was there when they needed him. When I asked the question as to whether it would be better to have a local leader, Ayann replied, "That is Kiogi's quality. It never felt to us that he was not physically with us, that he was in Brazil and we were in India. Every time by email,

phone, by any means we were trying to communicate, he was always
there and he was trying to help us."

India and Brazil have an eight-hour time difference between them,
so I wondered how Kiogi made this happen. Kiogi provided a summary
of his approach to his distant team.

> » "I gave priority to their requests, whether by phone, by chat, by email or any other channel (e.g. Facebook). The importance of answering them quickly was very clear and this helped to create the sense of closeness.

> » Shift my working hours. I started my work at 5:30am with a daily meeting with the team in India. In this way, we had an opportunity to be in touch every day.

> » Two trips to India during which I dedicated the work time during the day, and the social time at night, to create strong connections with the team and learn more about their culture. After my first trip, I prepared a video with pictures and video clips of our happy moments together and they loved it!

> » Birthdays. On each birthday of the team members, I always sent greetings, taking the opportunity to show gratitude for their dedication. "

In spite of the 14,000-kilometer distance, the team in India felt close
to Kiogi. The team are an example of how intentional actions can lead
to the feeling of perceived closeness.

Inclusion

One implicit theme that weaves itself throughout the fabric of this book is
that of inclusiveness. Global virtual teams can be defined by their cultural
diversity, and most likely other types of diversity as well, such as gender,

function, age and experience. But simply bringing people together does not guarantee that the benefits will be realized. It is through inclusiveness that the whole team feel like they belong, that they can all make a positive contribution and that everyone is valued for their uniqueness.

One of my favorite *Harvard Business Review* articles is by David A. Thomas and Robin J. Ely, titled "Making Differences Matter: A New Paradigm for Managing Diversity."[6] In this oft-cited article, the authors make a distinction between three types of diversity paradigms in organizations.

1. The Discrimination and Fairness Paradigm. Thomas and Ely state that the underlying mindset of this paradigm is that "we are all the same or aspire to be all the same." In their quest for fairness, leaders may lose sight of the unique qualities of each culture and person. Their approach is a 'one size fits all' perspective, and generally they want everyone to conform to the standard approach. They see disagreement based on different backgrounds as difficult and undesirable for team harmony.

   This paradigm is evident when a successful US firm expands in Germany and assumes that the German consumers have the same buying preferences and habits as the Americans.

2. The Access and Legitimacy Paradigm. In this paradigm, Thomas and Ely observe that leaders view diversity as a means to achieve objectives. For instance, when the team creates products for Japanese clients, then they need a Japanese market expert on the team. In their practical approach, the other team members may overlook the opportunity to learn about a new culture. Also, the Japanese team member is assigned the role of expert, but then ignored when the team discusses other topics.

3. The Emerging Paradigm: Connecting Diversity to Work Perspectives. Thomas and Ely describe organizations with this paradigm as

140

acknowledging the cultural diversity and striving for integration of everyone's perspective. The team actively learns and grows because of the differences. As the authors write in the article, "We are all on the same team, with our differences-not despite them."

The team members of the team with the Japanese clients would all actively be learning about Japan and the culture, not only to serve the client but also to expand their understanding of how people live and work. When the team discusses topics that are not related to the Japanese market, the opinion of the Japanese colleague is welcomed as a perspective that is different from that of the others.

Thomas and Ely list preconditions of making the paradigm shift for organizations. I have applied the spirit of the preconditions to leaders of multicultural virtual teams. The leader:

- Believes in the benefits of diversity and values diverse background, opinions and insights.
- Recognizes the learning opportunities and challenges on culturally diverse teams, and invests the time and energy to realize the benefits.
- Expects everyone to perform at high standards, regardless of background.
- Advocates for personal development through training, coaching and other methods so that each person, regardless of their background, has a chance to grow.
- Encourages open conversations and perspective sharing.
- Genuinely values each employee and what they contribute to the team.
- Aligns the team around the shared purpose and goals as a means to unite the diversity.

- Welcomes and encourages new ideas and ways of working.

Inclusive leadership behavior on global virtual teams ultimately has an impact on team performance. The inclusive leader, however, knows the starting place for guiding the team begins with herself and her view of cultural diversity.

Perspective Taking

A diverse team has the potential for creativity, but it requires more than simply showing up on a team. What is the mystery ingredient that makes 1+1=3 a true equation? The commonly spoken formula that conveys the idea that people who are working together can create and deliver more than if they worked alone. One answer is perspective taking, and I do not mean just imagining what colleagues might think. I mean active inquiry based on curiosity and learning. And the team leader plays a crucial role in whether a diverse team is creative.

To explain how a leader can help create an environment where creativity thrives from the diversity of ideas, I will reference the flow in Figure 7.1, but I will not follow the order of the flow, because I want to start with the critical activity, active perspective taking.

Figure 7.1 How Perspective Taking Leads to Creativity

Active Perspective Taking

I discovered the concept of perspective taking when I read the paper with the irresistible title "Fostering Team Creativity: Perspective Taking as Key to Unlocking Diversity's Potential," written by four authors, including Professor Inga Hoever of Erasmus University in Rotterdam.[7]

Hoever found that when diverse teams actively engage in perspective taking, they outperform homogeneous teams in terms of creativity and innovation.[8] As I read the work and interviewed her for this book, it became clear that successful perspective taking does not happen automatically but depends on the mindset of the colleagues and generative dialogue.

Let's imagine that you and I meet for the first time and we are from different countries. We agree to have dinner together. For you, that is an elaborate four-course meal because this is your big meal for the day. For me, it is a small soup and salad because my big meal was at lunch. We have different perspectives on a concept. We also assume the other has the same view of dinner, because, we each apply our own cultural assumptions. We don't really consider that it could be something else than our own understanding of 'dinner.'

Substitute the word 'customers' for 'dinner.' We meet via video to discuss a solution for regional customers. We each start to speak about the customers in our countries, and the type of solutions they need. The problem with our normal way of speaking is that we assume that the other person knows what we are talking about. Afterall, when I speak to someone in my own location, they know what I mean by 'dinner' and by 'customer.' But when you and I speak, we may have a knowledge gap. We simply do not have the same references.

Since we do not have the same references, this gap can become an opportunity. When you are learning from me and I am learning from you, it helps both of us to reframe our understanding of a situation. Also, if your ideas intersect with my ideas, it may lead to innovative thinking and solutions.

The Role of the Team Leader

Professor Hoever's work only looked at perspective taking, and the work of Professors van Knippenberg, van Ginkel and Homan provided insights into how the team leader can play a crucial role in the perspective taking practices of the team.[9] Based on their work, team leaders can support their team in three ways:

Attitude: Does the team leader believe that the diversity on the team is an advantage that can lead to learning and creativity? Does he advocate for the diversity in the team and share his vision of the potential?

Behaviors and activities: The team leader allocates the time and organizes activities for the team members to participate in active perspective taking. Some examples are:

- During meetings, the team leader asks each team member to elaborate on their perspective and inquires to understand the context of each team member's point of view.
- The team leader regularly encourages the team members to view a situation from another's point of view.
- The team leader organizes presentations so that one colleague gives the viewpoint of the other. Through this activity, the colleague must learn more than superficially what the other thinks.
- The team leader structures the task assignments so that diverse colleagues work together on shared goals. Through the collaboration, they learn more about each other's point of view.

- The team leader rotates the role of meeting note-takers so that team members summarize the ideas of their colleagues.
- The team leader organizes theme meetings in which each person shares their perspective on a topic. The team leader can use trigger questions to help the team members realize they need to provide more than superficial explanations.

Reflection and learning: The team leader facilitates conversations within the team about the experience of perspective taking. For instance, when is the team at its best, when is perspective taking necessary or not, what has worked well and what can be improved? In addition, how each team member experiences the perspective taking process with the others. Through moments of reflection on how the team leverages the diversity, the team can actively engage in their own learning process.

Perspective Taking is Tiring

This takes effort. As Hoever explained, "There is some brain research that shows that perspective taking is one of the more cognitively taxing things that we can engage in because it takes a lot of mental energy. This would suggest that humans don't do it readily all the time." But teams can use active perspective taking when they need to create and innovate.

Perspective taking is an advantageous way to shine a spotlight on the assumptions that drive our points of view and behaviors. This chapter highlights that perspective taking is not simply imagining the other person's point of view, but active inquiry with curiosity and openness. Through the conversations, virtual team members often bridge the physical distance with learning, sharing and respect.

Key Points

- The technological infrastructure of the virtual team can decrease the feeling of human contact. Virtual teams need to actively bring in humanity to their collaboration.
- Team members can care for each other from a distance, and need to do so as the virtuality can cause team members to feel disconnected.
- Team members can feel close to each other, called perceived proximity, and is a result of communication and shared identity.
- Given the cultural diversity of the team, team inclusion becomes a critical goal and requires intentional efforts.
- When giving feedback, virtual team leaders must realize they probably have less information than if they were giving feedback to a co-located colleague. This means they should start the feedback session with the intention of understanding the situation in order to more effectively give feedback that makes sense to the feedback receiver.
- Instead of imagining the perspective of another person, active perspective taking is more accurate and results in more creative teams. Active perspective taking is a means of respecting the other colleagues and including their point of view.
- Global working invites us to be present 24/7, but we need to decline the invitation. Global knowledge workers enjoy the benefits of virtual work when they have time to recover.

CHAPTER 8

Complete the Work

The fourth Leadership Lever, Complete the Work, focuses on how the team actually communicate and collaborate as a team. The majority of this chapter is focused on the use of communication and collaboration technology, as that is the backbone of virtual working. How a team uses the technology can have an impact on the efficiency of the team. Also in this chapter is research about influencing virtually, as many people wonder how to influence from a distance, in the absence of the lunches and informal meetings that often help to sway someone or get them on board. In this chapter, I also put a microscope on conflict, and identify three types, some desirable and some not.

This is the fourth and final Leadership Lever. As the reader closes this part of the book, I hope the reader feels empowered to support their team to make the shift for higher engagement, performance and satisfaction.

Structure to Leverage the Flexibility

Remote working could be defined as the ultimate in flexibility because teams can work wherever, whenever and with whomever they want. However, virtual teams benefit from structure to ensure the flexibility doesn't stray into chaos.

Some may think that too much structure will strangle the energy for creativity and agility. On the contrary, as Professors Line Dubé and Daniel Robey of HEC Montréal and Georgia State University, respectively, concluded from their interviews with multiple virtual teams in various businesses. "To reap the benefits of flexibility required a great deal of structure in communication and processes, potentially threatening the creativity, innovation and rapid response to organizational threats or opportunities. The challenge was to support flexibility through structural mechanisms that coordinated team efforts."[1] The advice was to create the structure and adapt it when the situation had changed.

Below are examples of building a structure for the team, which can support their way of working:

- Standardization of documentation and communication processes
- Team rhythm of meetings and celebrations, including one-on-one meetings
- Clear deliverables with deadlines and accountability
- Methodology for completing the work together; the team may follow a certain project management or agile methodology
- Agreement on which communication tools to use for which task
- Practice for informing the team of new information, developments and decisions that keep everyone informed in a timely manner

Each team will create its own structure depending on organizational norms and the team context. As the structure and practices are in place, regularly check to ensure that it still serves the team in a way that allows them to perform well.

Team Rhythm

Just like a rhythm keeps dancers moving to the same beat, a regular rhythm helps a virtual team work together. In virtual teams, a rhythm refers to the regular meetings and interactions that are time based. For instance, the morning stand-up, the biweekly team meetings, the weekly project updates and the monthly one-on-ones are all examples of time-based interactions. The regular rhythm helps the team members to feel connected and pumps energy into the team processes.

Team members need organized reminders that they are part of a team. Co-located teams have the advantage of seeing each other regularly and meeting for informal lunches, all of which help them to identify with the team. Because virtual teams have fewer physical interactions and reminders within their surroundings, regular, predictable points of contact can fill the gap. These events become the moments to positively recognize the existence of the team, reinforce commitments and revive feelings of connection with their distant colleagues. The team rhythm provides continuity and long-term stability in a continuously changing environment of many virtual teams.

The beats of connection may be synchronous or asynchronous. A common beat is a synchronous video team meeting. If the team is widely geographically spread, the beat may be a 24-hour asynchronous chat meeting, in which everyone contributes during their working hours.

Your team's beat will be very unique. The team rhythm reinforces the team identity and helps the team to move together.

Technology

When I ask people why they don't like to turn on the video to speak with their colleagues, the number one reason is, "I don't like to see myself on the screen." This aversion to looking at ourselves is common. Fortunately, some creators of video software have taken this human condition into account and offer a 'hide self' feature.

The technology may be sophisticated, but we are still humans using it, with our egos, emotions and impatience.

Fortunately, communication technology has improved exponentially over the past years and it will continue to improve. The whiz kids of the tech world are offering many programs and solutions with the bells and whistles to communicate, monitor, share and connect. For those with access to speed and bandwidth, the world is at their fingertips.

Technology brings people together but can also add stress to their lives. Employees can be available 24/7 and, depending on the corporate culture of the company, may be expected to respond-even on vacation. A Rand-stad US study found, "A majority of employers (53%) expect employees to at least sometimes respond to business messages while on vacation."[2]

The most damaging issue with collaboration via technology is that we may lose our humanity. An email address does not give an indication as to the type of person sara1973@jones.com might be. We read the text and forget the human. We also are likely to misinterpret emotions when reading emails, thereby reacting on the wrong impression.[3]

Colleagues risk miscommunication if they only use email. Surprisingly, emoticons can help. Researchers found that the cute little smiles, frowns, winks and hearts activate parts of the brain and are like nonverbal communication.[4] But note, they are best used at the end of a sentence to add some emotional clarity.

Fortunately, users can send more and more clues across the communication tools. Colleagues can see facial expressions, hear voices and look at pictures. But they cannot hug, touch, smell or feel one's presence. Virtual communicators are not using all of their senses. This means that technology encourages users to focus on tasks, agendas and solutions at the expense of the humanity, relationship and connection, the very elements that build trust, empathy and compassion. It is not surprising then, that many people do not feel connected with their distant colleagues. To feel connected means to feel an emotion toward a colleague, which is something more than knowing how well they have completed their assigned task. It means knowing their dreams, what makes them laugh and what makes them feel stressed.

To feel connected also means that my colleagues know these things about me. As humans, we want to be understood.

Communication technology is the means for colleagues to connect on a virtual team; it is a defining presence. In this section, I show how to leverage the technology by focusing on the human connections and creating the environment for exceptional collaboration.

Technology Definitions

Communication tools come in many shapes and sizes and have certain benefits and disadvantages. By distinguishing the tools, the users can then decide which tools to use for the appropriate task.

Synchronous communication means in real time and refers to communication in which the sender and receiver are actively engaged at the same moment. When we meet for a virtual coffee on video we have synchronous communication. I hear you at the same time you speak, and I can respond immediately. Other examples are phone, video meetings and teleconferences. The advantages of synchronous communication are clarity, and the chance for immediate follow-up questions. The disadvantages are scheduling everyone to be present at the same time and the lack of documentation (unless everyone agrees to record the interaction).

Asynchronous communication, by contrast, means not at the same time and has a delay. You write an email, and I read it two hours later. I respond, and then you read my email the next day. Communication does not happen in real time and most likely experiences a delay. The advantages of asynchronous communication are flexibility and brevity. We do not have to schedule anything, and sometimes a quick answer is all that is needed. Another advantage is documentation and the famous email trail. Other asynchronous tools include text, WhatsApp, chat groups and blogs.

An additional distinction is the intention of the communication:[5]

Conveyance communication process means information must be passed from one person to another (or many) and read, digested and understood by the receiver. Interaction between the receiver and sender is not necessary in the moment of communication. Examples are the sending of a new travel policy in a company, or a webinar that explains a new way of using a certain chemical in a product.

Convergence communication process means the sender(s) and receiver(s) are bringing their ideas together, perhaps to clarify the meaning of information or to create something new. They discuss back and forth, listening, explaining, and end the dialogue with a general understanding of positions and/or solutions. Examples are brainstorming sessions, conflict resolution meetings or project planning meetings.

In general, the more convergence that is necessary in the communication, the higher will be the need for synchronous communication. For instance, decision-making by email may be efficient, but it can also be prone to miscommunication and uncertainty. This would be a good moment to use tools in which everyone can hear the other person, voice their opinions, ask questions for clarification and make the decision. A telephone conference or video conference would be the best choice. The final decision can then be confirmed through asynchronous communication such as email, shared company websites and chat channels.

Task-Technology Fit

Armed with the categories of communication tools, it is time to agree which tools to use for what purpose. First we will consider tools in general and then add the cultural flavor to the mix.

In general, a team with more variety of functionality in their tools will have a higher team performance because team members have more resources to communicate and coordinate the tasks. On the other hand, teams struggle when they have multiple tools to do the same thing. It helps if the team reaches agreement on which tools will be used to support their structure for communication and coordination.

As your team considers the different options, you can adapt Figure 8.1 and complete with your team.

Below are general considerations for this chart and can be a starting point for your team as they determine the best task-technology fit.

- **Data Sharing.** Email or team document site are generally used for data sharing. Team members can read the documents when they want.
- **Project Update.** Regular project updates are usually the cause of boring meetings where participants think 'this could have been an email.' Efficient project updates can be a two-step process. First, using an asynchronous tool such as chat or a project update tool, team members can update the team. During the synchronous team meetings, instead of updates, team members discuss issues or key learnings.
- **Quick Question.** Generally, quick questions can be through phone or personal message (if the person is available), more synchronous tools. Email is not appropriate because the quick question will be lost in a full email box.

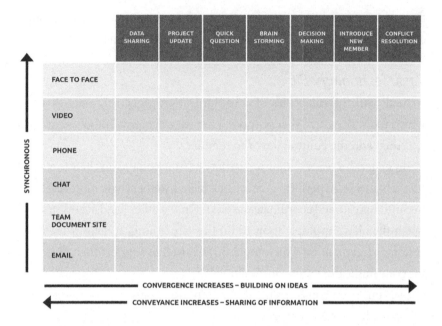

Figure 8.1 Task-Technology Fit Team Discussion Guide

- **Brainstorming.** Often brainstorming is considered an event with post-it notes and flip charts. When working virtually, teams can approach brainstorming in two ways. Firstly, the use of software specifically for brainstorming and generating new ideas. Some tools allow for anonymous contributions, which can minimize *groupthink*. Secondly, to consider the creation of new ideas as a process and not an event. In this case, all the tools would be used, such as to share research on a team document site, discuss the findings in a video meeting and comment on new directions in a chat group.

- **Decision-Making.** The more critical the decision, the more reason to use synchronous tools such as phone or video. Decision-making is a convergence communication process, which requires clarity, alignment and shared commitment. Particularly on multicultural virtual teams, even a brief video meeting can improve the quality of the final decision process.

- **Conflict Resolution.** In spite of the fact that there is sometimes nothing better than putting your frustrations in an email and hitting send, we all know that the probability of this action ending in a disaster and a string of *mea culpas* is high. Whenever an email begins with 'you don't understand' or 'that is not what I meant,' it is time to pick up the phone, or turn on the video and have a person-to-person synchronous conversation.

Each team is different in the types of tools they have access to and how they use them. Teams who discuss the task-technology fit eliminate the uncertainty of how to communicate and tend to be more efficient in their communication practices.

Media Richness

The previous section described the foundations of the communication tools, but the experience of the communication tools can change over time. To explore this, I reference the concept of 'media richness,' which gives an indication of how well a communication tool communicates complex tasks by sending information and cues. When a team begins a project, the tools it uses can easily fit along a spectrum indicating their so-called richness, such as in Figure 8.2.

As teams work together and learn about each other, the media richness of a tool can increase. If I receive an email from a new client, I have fewer informational cues than an email from a trusted colleague. Because of our relationship, the trusted colleague sends more meaning and cues in the email.

Media richness is important to consider when a team is trying to create a spirit of copresence, where they feel connected in spite of the geographic

LOW   HIGH

EMAIL   CHAT   PHONE   VIDEO   FACE
                                CONFERENCE   TO FACE

Figure 8.2 Media Richness

distance. In this case, they should use the richest media tools available such as video meetings. Over time as the team know each other, they may sometimes choose to use the phone, for instance, as this has become a tool which conveys more meaning.[6]

The richness of the type of media a team has chosen can also convey an unconscious message to each other. As mentioned in Chapter Three, section Between the Locations, as humans, we tend to view people at a distance as more abstract than those nearby. One signal that influences the level of psychological distance is the communication tool that a person chooses to use. If a person selects a tool that is less rich, then he sends a signal that he wants to maintain the distance. He wants to speak only about tasks, deliverables, agendas, and not become closer to the other. For instance, if a team can use video when meeting, but they choose to keep the video off, then they are sending a signal that they want to maintain the psychological distance and avoid the deeper, vulnerable conversations that builds trust and gives meaning to the collaboration.

The first step for a team is to agree on which tools to use and then to revisit this agreement regularly. When a team is struggling to have meaningful conversations, one place to look would be the communication tools that they use.

Culture and Communication Tools

Early in my relationship with my Dutch husband, I found it difficult to understand the English words that he was saying. I was continuously asking "What did you say?" and I wondered to myself whether I could marry a man whom I really could not understand. Over time, my ears adjusted to his accent and I could understand him, especially when he said "I do."

Experienced global teams realize that clear communication across cultures can be challenging. Not only do we have cultural assumptions, but there are also accents and different interpretations of the same word. Professors Klitmøller and Lauring of Aarhus University, studied 14 global teams in a large Danish multinational company.[7] The teams consisted of various configurations of Danish and Indian members. From a cultural point of view, these two countries are very different. For instance, Denmark is more individualistic than the collectivist India. India has a more diffuse communication style, whereas Danish are more direct and to the point. One thing that they did have in common was that English was a second language for everyone. Some of the findings of the study were:

- The Danish complained of the long emails explaining everything from the Indian team members. The Indian team members found the Danish emails much too short, without enough explanation, causing them to follow up with questions.
- Both teams commented on the accents or language proficiency of the other and inability to understand each other. During a video conference, the Indians used the word 'shot blasting' and the Danes understood 'sand blasting,' which could have resulted in costly process errors.
- The meaning of 'yes' is ambiguous. The Indian team used it as a sign of respect, or that the message has been heard. The Danish team assumed agreement.
- Both teams liked tools in which they could write. They could

reflect on what they wanted to say, double check the language and sometimes ask colleagues to review the written word for accuracy of content.

In the section Task-Technology Fit, I suggested that the more complex the conversation, the richer the media because it can provide more cues from the speakers. But this research turns that advice on its head. They found that advice was not always effective. The richer the media, the more the chance of confusion. A video call to explain complex manufacturing technical issues left both teams puzzled in the end. A helpful solution was to use email or chat to document some of the most complex issues and then follow up with video. Also, sometimes the teams used phone calls to agree on dates of meetings, which normally could be done in the calendar tool. This scheduling conversation provided a welcome moment of understanding amongst all the communication challenges.

This reminds me of a conversation I had with Hiroji, a Japanese manager located in Tokyo. He often had meetings with colleagues in Sweden, and he realized that they simply had two different expectations for that virtual meeting. The Swedes arrived ready to discuss and make decisions. As the Swedes are generally very proficient in English, the company language, they were comfortable with the words they used. The Japanese colleagues, on the other hand, viewed the meeting as a chance to share information and understanding, but they were absolutely not ready to commit to decisions. They wanted to discuss issues with their local colleagues to clarify the impact of the decision and get their buy-in ahead of time. And just as important, they wanted to reflect on what they heard and take the time to select words that expressed their points of view. They wanted to write an email for clarity because they were not confident of the words they would use in a fast-paced meeting environment.

Both of these examples highlight how the variety of communication tools can be used to explain, discuss, answer, confirm and reinforce. Multicultural teams can look at their communication risk points and consider using different tools to ensure that messages have been sent and received as intended.

Cognitive Load

When people speak a language in which they are not fluent or highly proficient, they may experience cognitive load, meaning that their brain uses extra energy. The cognitive load from speaking a second language can happen during virtual meetings, chat rooms or conference calls. It is tiring, and the translating process can use brain processing power so that less content is understood and stored in memory.

Multicultural teams select asynchronous tools to reduce the cognitive load. It is simply easier for them to communicate, check, review and also to read and understand. The thinking, listening and deciding is heavy work in another language. Also, allowing team members to speak their own language to confirm their understanding is not a way to exclude the rest of the team, but to lighten the cognitive load so that they can participate with greater understanding.

Professors Tenzer and Pudelko of University of Tuebingen found that people would rather have less cognitive load and take more time with more and different communication tools than have to make a decision right at that moment.[8]

As a German participant in their study explained, "I sometimes think about an English e-mail for quite a long time until I have formulated it carefully enough to be sure that the other person can understand what I have written. The best way is certainly to write an e-mail and then call the person ten minutes later: 'I wrote you an e-mail, is everything in it clear? This is what it is about.' Then I notice if the other person understood what I wanted to say."

Multicultural teams benefit from the quick exchange of video and audio combined with the cognitive relief of written communication. This may mean that some communication is repeated, or followed up for understanding. One conversation may not bring clarity to everyone. Part of working virtually successfully is realizing the impact of different language capabilities and developing strategies to understand each other.

Who is Responsible for Communication?

An Account Manager located in Argentina, with R&D colleagues in China, explained how she approached using communication tools. "The Chinese colleagues don't really check every email. It is a very different concept because for Argentina they will think, 'Ok, I did my part and sent the email. If you did not read the email and you did not receive the message or information, that is your fault, because you are responsible to read every email.' Chinese colleagues think 'I am so busy, I have 600 emails in my main box and most of them are not important. So how can you expect me to read every email? If it is really urgent, why didn't you call me?' So now, when I send an email to them, I also send a screen shot in WhatsApp of that email if it needs to be done sometime today. If it is super urgent, then I will send the email and call right away."

Influencing Virtually

Influence. We do it all the time, even if we are not aware of it. We influence our children to clean their rooms, our partners to visit our parents on the weekend and our friends to meet at our favorite restaurant. At work we continue our influencing behaviors when we request a colleague to attend an important meeting or ask the headquarters to increase the department budget by 25%. I am trying to influence you through this book using rational arguments and inspirational appeals.

Professionals who contemplate and research the topic of influence can list various types, such as direct pressure (words that clearly demand and threaten), legitimizing (using one's authority for the request) and coalition building (working with others to influence the target). In this chapter, we will look at how to influence others who are geographically far away.

In co-located environments, the three most common influencing techniques are rational arguments, ingratiation and coalitions.[9] Rational arguments use data and other facts to show how the proposal can make a difference to reach certain outcomes. Influencers use ingratiation when they use their relationship to appeal to the influencer by making them feel good about the request. For instance, taking a colleague to lunch to convince them to join a project is an example of ingratiation.

Influencers use coalitions when they recognize that doing it alone is not enough. Not only can colleagues in a coalition add more thinking power to the proposal but they can also use their connections to broaden the network.

These influencing techniques work effectively when people are co-located and share the same cultural cues and understanding of the local context. Team members can also meet in person where they can use a warm handshake and smile to win someone over or a harsh stare to put pressure.

Influencing virtually is different than influencing co-located both in type and degree. Virtual influencers lose many of the communication and cultural cues of their co-located counterparts and therefore need to think differently about how to influence colleagues and other stakeholders.

Generally, the preferred styles of influencing virtually are rational arguments, coalition and intermediary, particularly when trying to influence upward in the hierarchy.[10] Notice that ingratiation, preferred when co-located, drops off the list. It is very difficult to use personal charm to convince from a distance. Instead, people increase their use of rational argument with links, data and charts.

As mentioned, influencers use intermediaries more when working virtually than when co-located. An intermediary is a person who is somehow connected with the person to be influenced, and therefore can help the influencer to solidify his position. Specifically, intermediaries can help the influencer understand the situation, the communication preferences and other characteristics of the person to be influenced. They may even directly help with the influencing process.

Virtual Intermediaries in Action

Tony, Head of e-Commerce at a major Nordic bank, provides an example of using intermediaries: "Last year I had to run a project and cooperate with someone from a different organization. He was in Sweden, I in Denmark, and we had to work together on this big project. We had very different working styles and we disagreed on many things. We were both mature enough to recognize it, but it added to the difficulties. I was trying to get my points through in all the different ways that I could. I tried speaking directly with him with reason, but that did not work. Their department is also distributed, so they have people in all locations. At the time, I committed myself to sit physically together with their people in Denmark at least once a week. I discussed my issue with the Danish crew and tried to find some allies. When I sat with them, I had the opportunity to explain the situation and asked them if they could speak to their Swedish colleagues and explain my position, which they did. I was able to get the changes that I needed."

Eliminating Ambiguity

People trying to influence across cultures and virtually may have an extra

162

complication because the stakeholder that they want to influence does not know the culture or context and therefore does not really understand the request. To address this issue, Professors Wadsworth and Blanchard, of the University of North Carolina, found an interesting tactic used by virtual influencers that is less common in co-located teams, which they called eliminating ambiguity.[11] Eliminating ambiguity is an empathetic approach by the influencer to decrease the confusion of the person to be influenced and to help them become more at ease with the request. This differs from the purely rational argument, which is basically the same whether virtual or co-located. For example, they share additional information, show examples and send pictures and videos to describe the request and help the distant person to be influenced to understand the entire situation.

Email to Open a Door

Email can play a role in the influencing process. Even though it is a words-based communication tool, users can add exclamation points to get someone's attention or emoticons to soften a request. Email senders can include supervisors on copy to increase the pressure on the email reader. More importantly, though, it provides an open door for someone's request or point of view. Often people will write their opening request in an email, which allows them to find the right words and ensure clarity of their rational. Once that email is sent, often they will follow up with a phone call or video call. This two-step process was found to be common, particularly in requests to managers or other senior stakeholders.

Virtual Influencing Breakthrough

Often, virtual managers use more than one influencing technique, as Li-yang did when he had to influence the CEO of a newly acquired company located in Norway. Li-yang, based in Amsterdam, was an

HR manager for a global organization with headquarters in Taipei. He was responsible for implementing management policies and an HR system as part of the post-acquisition integration plan. He knew that the CEO of the acquired company was frustrated by what he perceived as a tsunami of changes without his oversight. Li-yang needed to tread carefully.

"I was responsible for the project and needed to influence the manager of the local team, who was the CEO, which was not easy. I understood the policies and system, but I have a junior position, and it may not have been enough. I discussed this with my manager in Taipei and we arranged for a more senior HR Director to travel to Norway and give a presentation to the CEO. She explained the purpose and the logic behind the policies and system and how they fit in the big picture of the whole group. I was able to follow-up with the details and explained what this meant to them as a new company in our organization. After that, things went quite smoothly for this project. We implemented the system from Norway, Taipei and Amsterdam, managing the team virtually."

Li-yang used both rational arguments and intermediary influencing techniques, especially leveraging the hierarchical relationships to give credibility and show respect.

Conflict

When it comes to conflict in virtual teams, the findings of Professor Lindred Greer, of Stanford University, may raise alarms. She warned, "Conflict in virtual teams is more likely to be negative for performance and is more likely to escalate."[12]

According to Professor Greer, disagreements in virtual teams can escalate more quickly than in co-located teams because colleagues in conflict are more likely to take things personally with people they rarely see. The conflicting parties do not know the context of the other person and are therefore more likely to misinterpret information and communication style and also tend to quickly jump to erroneous conclusions. The lack of personal connection and uncertainty may cause people to be more aggressive in their response as compared to when people are together and are calmed by the human contact. With this prognosis, a team leader would want to focus on prevention of conflict to avoid unnecessary and detrimental disputes.

The Meaning of Conflict

The word *conflict* has many meanings, and everyone has their own emotional response to the word. To understand conflict, I will use three common distinctions of types of conflict, which are *relationship*, *process* and *task* conflicts.

Relationship conflict: Relationship conflict is when team members are incompatible and have a negative emotional reaction to each other. On a global team with different nationalities, cultural misunderstandings can be interpreted as relationship conflict. Relationship conflicts can be sinister because team members may feel animosity toward a colleague and use sabotage to express their annoyance. For example, Joe does not like Carlos and blocks any initiatives suggested by Carlos, or always declines the meetings that Carlos tries to schedule.

Generally, relationship conflicts are detrimental to virtual team performance.

Process conflict: Process conflicts arise when team members have differences regarding how the work should be completed. Examples would include who should do the task, in what order the task should be done, timing and duration of team meetings and who should inform key stakeholders? We are not speaking about ideas *per se*, but about task assignments, communication patterns and team flow. Process conversations can go well until suddenly the dynamic changes and processes quickly unravel. Underlying process conflicts can be ignited by issues of status, expectations of expertise, unspoken frustrations and feelings of being slighted or ignored. For instance, I might complain about the timing of a meeting, but my real frustration is because Sue was able to attend the industry conference and I had to finish the unglamorous project documentation.

Generally, process conflicts are detrimental to virtual team performance.

Task conflict: Task conflict is when team members do not agree on what should be done to reach the team goals and deliverables. These disagreements include work content or task activities. If team members disagree on the tasks to reach the goal, they have the potential to strengthen each other's position and the resulting solution.

Generally, task conflicts can be beneficial for virtual team performance.

Task conflict, however, does not guarantee higher performance. Exploring the different points can result in relationship or process conflict. For instance, Mieke and David have different points of view because of their backgrounds and experiences, thereby resulting in a task conflict. As they begin to share their respective perspectives, David feels attacked by Mieke's direct communication style and Mieke does not like that David is contacting other stakeholders. Now we have relationship and process conflicts.

Conflict Minimization Techniques

The overall goal of these recommendations is to minimize the chance of relationship and process conflicts so that teams can engage with task conflict. Only then can the team engage in healthy task conflicts, thereby leading to optimal team performance.

Create Communication Pathways: Team members need clearly established communication pathways so that when issues arise, they can easily and proactively engage with each other and clear up any misunderstanding.[13] This book has included many suggestions on how to create these pathways, such as activities to build team relationships, coffee chats and using media-rich communication.

Build the Relationships: This has been a theme throughout the book. Often relationship conflicts arise because people do not know each other well, so they do not trust each other and assume ill intent. In global virtual teams in particular, team members may judge each other according to their own cultural norms and are confused by the other colleagues' behaviors. As the team know each other better, and learn about each other's cultures, they are more likely to avoid relationship conflict.

Agree on Processes Early: Global virtual teams likely consist of team members who have different ideas on how to work together as a team, which is often based on the norms of each person's cultural background. Teams can mitigate process risk by agreeing early in the team's collective journey on how they will work together. They should regularly review to check if the agreements are still applicable or need to be updated.

Engage the Location-Disadvantaged: As mentioned in the section titled Team Configuration, team members can be at a disadvantage due to the location of other team members, of the team leader and of the headquarters. This dynamic may result in both relationship and process conflicts. The team leader can create inclusive processes and activities that consider power, advantage and isolation.

Monitor and Moderate Conflict: The team leader has an important role in regard to the presence and resolution of conflict.[14] To begin with, she can be alert to brewing relationship or process conflicts and see how she can help the parties to address the issue before it becomes a conflict. This may take many forms such as coaching the team members, revisiting agreed team norms or engaging a team coach to support the team's development.

With regard to task conflict, the team leader can help the team to recognize the conflict and moderate the discussions so that the team members are voice their opinions, share ideas and ultimately learn from each other. Depending on the maturity of the team, this moderation role can be crucial for the team to realize their full potential.

Facilitate Conversation on Conflict: How conflict is perceived, addressed and resolved varies across different cultures. Global teams benefit from a facilitated conversation about conflict, how each team member experiences conflict and what their expectations are for resolution.

Conflict is not inevitable in virtual teams. By developing the team spirit, helping the team members to connect and implementing other actions mentioned above, the team leader can help the team to deal effectively with conflict.

Overlapping Time Zones

The persistent time zone differences add stress to a team for a few reasons:

- Team members want to speak synchronically (at the same time) with each other.
- Team members want a timely response from a colleague, instead of waiting for them to wake up and come online.
- Teams want to have meetings that include everyone at the same time.
- Team members need to work together at the same time.

If you recognize that one of the reasons above is applicable to your team, then my first suggestion is to challenge the assumption. Perhaps the work or meetings can be restructured or reorganized.

Even with that in mind, synchronous communications are still desirable on a virtual team. Here are some examples of addressing the time differences.

Flex the working hours. The team or organization has a time zone, and everyone adjusts locally to work those hours. For instance, Karen, HR Director, explained how this works for her 100% remote company.

"I hire for a specific time zone, but they do not have to live in that time zone. They just need to be willing to work the hours of that time zone. My head of sales and marketing is in Turkey, but she works Eastern Standard Time hours because she is used to doing it and she gets better bandwidth at night."

Often, shared service centers allow flex time depending on the countries that the associates are supporting. They ensure a five-hour overlap with the service country. Another example was a European/Indian agile team in which the team in India began at 11:00 am, or 7:30 am European Central Time. The team had many people who used the morning time to care for their children. People wanted to join the team!

Use and jam-pack the overlapping working hours. The overlapping working hours are the golden moments for quick responses, full-attendance meetings, simultaneous coworking and anything else that you want done quickly. Intentionally use the window of opportunity wisely.

Avoid pajama parties. One senior director told me a story about how she was invited to the team monthly meeting at 3:00 am… and she attended! The majority of the team was in the headquarters and she was a lone satellite working from home with a six-hour time difference. The organizer did not realize what he was doing when he sent the invitation. The first suggestion is awareness of time zone differences.

The time difference between China and New York is 12 hours. A meeting is not within anyone's time zone unless someone flexes their time. The first question to answer is if the synchronous meeting necessary is really necessary. Can asynchronous communication meet the same objectives?

A global team with this issue realized that their global meetings were pajama parties for the sleepy Asians and Americans while the Europeans sat comfortably at work. The leader of the team was at the headquarters in Europe. Instead of one monthly meeting, they split the meeting into two meetings on the same day. The first meeting was during the Asian working hours, and the second meeting was during the working hours in the Americas, both of which overlapped with the European working hours. The Europeans shared information and received ideas from each meeting and documented the information so that everyone had access. They noticed a significant increase in the quality of the contributions from their Asian and American colleagues. We think and communicate better when we are awake.

Someone is waiting for you. Erik's company is located in the center of the Netherlands (headquarters) and Thailand (sales office), with a five-hour time zone difference. As he explained, "The Thai team are working in their morning, and need an answer or information. They send an email to the Dutch office, and wait. The Dutch come to work, have coffee with their colleagues, share the events of the evening, and then eventually answer the email. By the time they get around to the email it is 15.00 Thai time, for an email they sent a few hours before. They have been waiting all that time." All team members should understand the work-flow of their remote colleagues and adapt their work activities to ensure answers keep flowing.

Plan what you need, know whom you need it from and when you need it. There is nothing worse than needing a quick response from someone when they are sound asleep and you are halted on your work process. The story of the Norwegian who sent an email at 3:00 pm, his local time, to his Indian colleagues as they were leaving the office is frustrating for people in both locations. As you plan your day, consider the information or decisions you will need while your remote colleagues are still at work.

Time zone differences are the bane of a virtual team. However, with planning and asynchronous communication, teams can still communicate and collaborate effectively together.

Key Points

- A well-thought structure in a team can provide the foundation for the inherent flexibility to thrive instead of becoming chaos.
- A team rhythm of meetings and other moments that bring the team together can help team members to feel the team spirit and connection with each other.
- Virtual teams can agree on which tools to use for specific tasks, thereby eliminating confusion and improving communication efficiency.

- If the communicator wants to convey information, then generally asynchronous tools are appropriate.
- If the communicator wants to converge their ideas with other people, then generally synchronous tools are appropriate.
- As team members build relationships with each other, the richness of the media improves. An email from a stranger has different cues than an email from a trusted colleague.
- When influencing virtually, influencers tend to use rational argument, coalition and intermediary.
- Virtual influencers help the person to be influenced to understand the context of the request. They recognize that the person may need more information than if they were co-located.
- Virtual leaders can minimize the chance of relationship conflict by helping the team members to know each other, including the cultural diversity on the team.
- Virtual leaders can minimize the chance of process conflict by agreeing early in the team formation as to how the team will work together and reviewing the agreement periodically.
- Virtual leaders can encourage and facilitate task conflict when team members have different ideas of what needs to be done. These conversations can lead to creativity.
- Team members need to be aware of the time zone differences, especially overlapping working hours.

Conclusion

The need for knowledgeable, reflective and effective virtual leadership is essential in today's globalized economy. Organizations, and the people in them, have global ambitions and seek synergies in terms of customer reach, process efficiencies, product sourcing, access to talent and new innovations. But virtual work across borders is not only due to the whims of determined business avengers. We as a humanity face challenges that go beyond national borders such as climate change, pandemics and food insecurity. We need to be connected together to face these challenges and to find solutions on a global scale. Virtual working integrates the local and the global as locally based experts participate, share and create solutions in global forums, teams and organizations.

Team leaders who make the assumption that leading virtual teams is similar to leading co-located teams, just with more dependence on communication tools, will probably experience frustration and unrealized potential. Based on my own consulting practice, vast academic research and stories from the field, it is clear that leading and working virtually is different. This book has provided abundant evidence of the challenges and frustrations for virtual leaders. It has also provided success stories that demonstrate how managers can lead their teams to thrive in a virtual constellation and to deliver positive results in the real world.

Successful virtual leaders have the knowledge, competence, and mindset to lead multicultural virtual teams. They are reflective, caring, inclusive, supportive, visionary, creative, curious and results-oriented and they are excellent listeners and communicators. They are culturally competent and virtually competent. This may seem like a long list, but I have met numerous successful leaders who combine these characteristics into their leadership style.

Business is endlessly dynamic and transforming at a rapid pace. In this environment, speed, agility, innovation and excellence are the drumbeats towards high performance. The competences and capacities of knowledgeable and creative humans, not technology, will be a major differentiator and contribute to a competitive advantage. An underlying thread throughout this book has been the development of team leaders and members. The development comes in many forms such as training, mentoring, experimentation and new experiences. It is through the growth and development of the people that organizations can thrive in the fast-changing environment.

Technology companies will continue to offer new communication and collaboration platforms and solutions that help colleagues to see, hear and interact with each other. But the software engineers do not have a crystal ball to know how the users will experience the tools or give meaning to their experience. This is where practitioners like myself, academics and organizational professionals will continue to make a contribution. We will observe changes and support leaders and teams to be mindful and to understand their experience as they use the technology and work together from a geographic distance across cultures. Afterall, even though the technology is omnipresent, the humans are the ones who need to connect.

As mentioned in the introduction, I will continue to explore how geographic distance and cultural diversity impact the way people feel, think and act when working virtually across cultures. As I have done in this book, I am committed to reviewing the research in academia and verifying it with the reality of my clients and other organizations. If you would like to keep up to date, please read the blogs on my website www.interact-global.net or sign up for the newsletter there.

People purchase and sell, collaborate and create, and fall in love virtually across borders. I can imagine that we will continue to expand what we can do together, particularly as we realize that in order to address the global issues that we face , we need to overcome geographic and cultural borders. Only then can we reach our full potential for humanity.

Acknowledgements

Professor Surinder Kahai

When I began the journey to write this book, I wanted to partner with someone in academia who could provide the research regarding the leadership of virtual teams. Fortunately, Professor Surinder Kahai of Binghamton University was interested and we began our collaboration. In the first phase, Surinder was the guide as we reviewed and discussed various research topics. In the second phase, I was the guide as we interviewed people who I knew had an interesting story to tell. Surinder is a generous person with his time and ideas, and we both enjoyed the different perspectives we each brought to our conversations, particularly his academic view and my business view.

Unfortunately, the next phases of the book required time and energy, and Surinder was too busy with all the demands of an active, full-time professor. Even though I did the next phases by myself, I am very grateful for the start that I had with Surinder. He introduced me to the academic world and showed me how to navigate it. Our conversations were enriching as we respected each other's professions and tried to make meaningful connections between theory and practice. Thank you Surinder.

Many people have helped and supported me along the way. I cannot recognize them all, but want to put a special spotlight on certain people. My editor, book coach and friend Wendy Williams, who as an experienced author herself always knew the right words to say. For instance, the crucial words that pulled me out of the abyss, "Theresa, you are done researching, start writing."

Steve Harrison, who willingly read many academic papers and was the thought-provoking sounding board on many concepts that I was trying to clarify. Pilar Orti, who shared her experience as a published writer and

175

was always ready to give game-changing advice at different points in the process, as well as valuable edits.

To many people who supported me in a variety of ways:

Carolien Brinks, Larry Ebert, Michael Graham, Mark Kilby, Agnita Korsten, Tucker Miller, Monika Navandar, Jolanda Robinson Graham, Ryan Roghaar, Arien Scholtens, Li-yang Wang.

A special appreciation to all the professors and doctoral students who wrote papers that I read or referenced. A special thanks to all the people who graciously agreed to be interviewed. I was impressed by how open they were to reflect on their experience with me. Finally, to all the people whom I have met in workshops, coaching programs and other work engagements. Through our interactions, I have learned about myself, leadership and multicultural virtual teams.

About the Author

Theresa Sigillito Hollema has worked in and with global teams for over 25 years. As a cultural consultant and team facilitator, she has helped hundreds of leaders around the world learn how to excel when working with virtual, culturally diverse teams.

Theresa began her career in accounting and finance functions in the US, but always had an interest to work internationally. She took the chance on a short term assignment for a European based project and never looked back. She led programs and multicultural teams, particularly enjoying the post-merger integration work that crossed country borders. Theresa always found the cultural diversity in teams interesting and eventually turned her passion into a career.

Theresa joined Trompenaars Hampden-Turner, a leading cultural consulting firm, where she worked with teams and leaders from around the world. She is also trained as a team coach and has focused her attention on virtual work. Theresa now leads the team at InterAct Global, a group helping organizations capitalize on cultural diversity and virtual connections.

Theresa received her MBA from the University of Michigan in the US, including the Henry Ford II award for academic excellence.

Notes

Chapter One

1. O'Leary M. B. and Mortensen M. (2009) "Go (Con)figure: Subgroups, Imbalance, and Isolates in Geographically Dispersed Teams." *Organization Science* 21.1, pp. 115-131.

2. Bos N., Olson J., Nan N., Shami N.S., Hoch S. and Johnston E. (2006) "Collocation Blindness in Partially Distributed Groups: Is There a Downside to Being Collocated?" CHI 2006 Proceedings, *Computer-Mediated Communication.*

Chapter Two

1. Y2K means year of 2000, when most computer systems were expected to crash because they could not handle the date change from 1999 to 2000. Many people were on projects to implement new computer systems to solve this problem.

2. The dimension from the 7-Dimension model was Achievement-Ascription. In our story, this dimension gave an indication as to the importance of accomplishing something in each of our countries.

3. Trompenaars, F. (1993) *Riding the Waves of Culture: Understanding Diversity in Global Business*, 1st Edition, Nicholas Brealey Publishing Ltd.

4. Van der Kamp, M., Tjemkes B.V. and Jehn K.A. (2015) "Faultline Deactivation: Dealing with Activated Faultlines and Conflicts in Global Teams." *Leading Global Teams*, pp. 269-293, Springer.

5. DiStefano J. J. and Maznevski M.L. (2000) "Creating Value with Diverse Teams in Global Management." *Organizational Dynamics*, Vol. 29, No. 1, pp. 45–63.

6. Eisenberg J. and Mattarelli E. (2017) "Building Bridges in Global Virtual Teams: The Role of Multicultural Brokers in Overcoming the Negative Effects of Identity Threats on Knowledge Sharing Across Subgroups."

Journal of International Management, Vol. 23, No. 4, December pp. 399-411.

Chapter Three

1. Meyer E. (2014) *The Culture Map: Breaking Through the Invisible Boundaries of Global Business*. Public Affairs.

2. Hall E. T. (1976) *Beyond Culture*. Anchor Books..

3. Meyer E. (2014) *The Culture Map: Breaking Through the Invisible Boundaries of Global Business*. Public Affairs.

4. Trompenaars, F. (1993) *Riding the Waves of Culture: Understanding Diversity in Global Business,* 1st Edition, Nicholas Brealey Publishing Ltd.

5. Meyer E. (2014) *The Culture Map: Breaking Through the Invisible Boundaries of Global Business*. Public Affairs.

6. Trompenaars, F. (1993) *Riding the Waves of Culture: Understanding Diversity in Global Business,* 1st Edition, Nicholas Brealey Publishing Ltd.

7. Hofstede G. (1997) *Cultures and Organizations: Software of the Mind.* 1st. Edition, McGraw-Hill.

8. Trope Y. and Liberman N., (2010) "Construal-Level Theory of Psychological Distance." *Psychological Review*, 2010 Apr, 117(2), pp. 440–463.

9. Wilson J., Crisp C.B. and Mortensen M. (2013) "Extending Construal-Level Theory to Distributed Groups: Understanding the Effects of Virtuality." *Organization Science*, Vol. 24, No. 2.

10. Cramton C.D. and Hinds P.J. (2014) "An Embedded Model of Cultural Adaptation in Global Teams." *Organization Science*, Vol. 25, No. 4, pp. 1056–1081, INFORMS.

11. Per Institute of Actuaries in India, they had approx. 5400 members in 2018. Per Institute & Faculty of Actuaries in UK, they had approx. 30,000 members in 2016.

12. Presbitero A. and Toledano L.S. (2018) "Global Team Members' Performance and the Roles of Cross-Cultural Training, Cultural Intelligence, and Contact Intensity: The Case of Global Teams in IT Offshoring Sector." *The International Journal of Human Resource Management,* Vol 29. No. 14, pp. 2188-2208.

Chapter Four

1. Duhigg C., "What Google Learned From Its Quest to Build the Perfect Team," *New York Times*, February 25, 2016.

2. Breuer C., Hertel G. and Hüffmeier J. (2016) "Does Trust Matter More in Virtual Teams? A Meta-Analysis of Trust and Team Effectiveness Considering Virtuality and Documentation as Moderators." *Journal of Applied Psychology*, Vol. 101, No. 8, pp. 1151-1177.

3. Crisp C. B. and Jarvenpaa S. L. (2013) "Swift Trust in Global Virtual Teams: Trusting Beliefs and Normative Actions."*Journal of Personnel Psychology*, Vol.12 No. 1, pp. 45–56.

4. De Jong B. A., Dirks K. T. and Gillespie N. (2016) "Trust and Team Performance: A Meta-Analysis of Main Effects, Moderators and Covariates."*Journal of Applied Psychology*, Vol. 101 No. 8, pp. 1134–1150.

5. Cheng X., Yin G., Azadegan A. and Kolfschoten G. (2016) "Trust Evolvement in Hybrid Team Collaboration: A Longitudinal Case Study." *Group Decision and Negotiation*, Vol. 25, pp. 267-288, Springer Science+Business Media.

6. Duhigg C. "What Google Learned From Its Quest to Build the Perfect Team." *New York Times*, February 25, 2016.

7. Edmondson A.C. and Lei, Z. (2014) "Psychological Safety: The History, Renaissance, and Future of an Interpersonal Construct." *Annual Review of Organizational Psychology and Organizational Behavior,* Vol.1, No. 1,pp. 23-43..

8. Gibson C.B. and Gibbs J.L. (2006) "Unpacking the Concept of Virtuality: The Effects of Geographic Dispersion, Electronic Dependence,

Dynamic Structure, and National Diversity on Team Innovation." *Administrative Science Quarterly*, Vol. 51, No. 3, September, pp. 451-495.

9. Hinds P. J. and Mortensen M. (2005) "Understanding Conflict in Geographically Distributed Teams: The Moderating Effects of Shared Identity, Shared Context, and Spontaneous Communication, Organization Science." Vol. 16, No. 3, pp. 290-307.

Chapter Six

1. Josephs S.A. and Joiner W.B.(2006) *Leadership Agility: Five Levels of Mastery for Anticipating and Initiating Change.* John Wiley & Sons. The percentages in this paragraph were updated from the www.changewise.biz website..

2. Bell B. S. and Kozlowski S. W. J. (2002) "A Typology of Virtual Teams: Implications for Effective Leadership." *Group & Organization Management,* Vol. 27, No. 1, pp. 14–49.

3. Maynard T. and Gilson L.L (2014) "The Role of Shared Mental Model Development in Understanding Virtual Team Effectiveness." *Group and Organizational Management*, Vol. 39, No. 1, pp. 3-32.

4. Sivunen A. (2006) "Strengthening Identification with the Team in Virtual Teams: The Leaders' Perspective." *Group Decis Negot* Vol. 15, pp. 345–366.

5. Bos N., Olson J., Nan N., Sadat Shami N., Hoch S. and Johnston E. (2006) "Collocation Blindness in Partially Distributed Groups: Is There a Downside to Being Collocated." *Proceedings of the SIGCHI Conference on Human Factors in Computing Systems*, April, pp. 1313-1321.

6. Griffith T. and Neale M.A. (2001) "Information Processing and Performance in Traditional and Virtual Teams: The Role of Transactive Memory." *Research in Organizational Behavior*, Vol. 23, pp. 391.

7. Griffith T. and Neale M.A. (2001) "Information Processing and Performance in Traditional and Virtual Teams: The Role of Transactive Memory, Research in Organizational Behavior." Vol. 23, pp. 379-421.

8. Depping A.E., Mandryk R.L., Johanson C., Bowey J.T. and Thomson S.C. (2016) "Trust Me: Social Games are Better than Social Icebreakers at Building Trust." *Proceeding of the 2016 Annual Symposium on Computer-Human Interaction in Play* (CHI Play), pp. 116-129.

Chapter Seven

1. Purvanova R.K. and Bono J.E. (2009) "Transformational Leadership in Context: Face-to-Face and Virtual Teams." *The Leadership Quarterly*, Vol. 20, No. 3, pp. 343-357.

2. Nurmi N. and Hinds P.J. (2016) "Job Complexity and Learning Opportunities: A Silver Lining in the Design of Global Virtual Work." *Journal of International Business Studies*, No. 47, pp. 631-654.

3. Inspired by the book Lahey L.L. and Kegan R. (2000) *How the Way We Talk Can Change the Way We Work: Seven Languages for Transformation.* Jossey-Bass

4. Magni M., Ahuja M.K and Maruping L.M. (2018) "Distant but Fair: Intra-Team Justice Climate and Performance in Dispersed Teams." *Journal of Management Information Systems*, Vol. 35, No. 4, pp. 1031-1059.

5. O'Leary M.B., Wilson J.M. and Metiu A. (2012) "Beyond Being There: The Symbolic Role of Communication and Identification in the Emergence of Perceived Proximity in Geographically Dispersed Work." ESSEC Working Paper 1112.

6. Thomas D.A. and Ely R.J. (1996) "Making Differences Matter: A New Paradigm for Managing Diversity" *Harvard Business Review*, September-October.

7. Hoever I.J., van Knippenberg D., van Ginkel W.P. and Barkema H.G. (2012) "Fostering Team Creativity: Perspective Taking as Key to Unlocking Diversity's Potential."*Journal of Applied Psychology*, Vol 97 No. 5, pp. 982–996.

8. Hoever I.J. (2012) "Diversity and Creativity: In Search of Synergy."

Thesis to Obtain a Doctorate, Erasmus University. Promoter: Prof. Dr. D.L. van Knippenberg.

9. Van Knippenberg D., van Ginkel W.P. and Homan A.C. (2013) "Diversity Mindsets and the Performance of Diverse Teams." *Organizational Behavior and Human Decision Processes*, No. 121, pp. 183-193.

Chapter Eight

1. Dubé L. and Robey D. (2008) "Surviving the Paradoxes of Virtual Teamwork." *Information Systems Journal*, Vol. 19, pp. 3-30.

2. Randstad US, "Randstad US Study Reveals Ways Technology Has Helped (and Hurt) Us in the Workplace." blogpost, April 23, 2019, https://www.prnewswire.com/news-releases/randstad-us-study-reveals-ways-technology-has-helped-and-hurt-us-in-the-workplace-300836229.html.

3. Laubert C. and Parlamis J. (2019) "Are You Angry (Happy, Sad) or Aren't You? Emotion Detection Difficulty in Email Negotiation." *Group Decision and Negotiation*, Vol. 28 pp. 377-413.

4. Yuasa M., Saito K. And Mukawa N. (2011) "Brain Activity When Reading Sentences and Emoticons: An fMRI Study of Verbal and Nonverbal Communication." *Electronics and Communications in Japan*, Vol. 94, No. 5.

5. Dennis A., Fuller R.M. and Valacich J.S. (2008) "Media, Tasks and Communication Processes: A Theory of Media Synchronicity." *MIS* Q. 32, No. 3, pp., 575-600.

6. Dennis A., Fuller R.M. and Valacich J.S. (2008) "Media, Tasks and Communication Processes: A Theory of Media Synchronicity." *MIS* Q. 32, No. 3, pp., 575-600.

7. Klitmøller A. and Lauring J. (2013) "When Global Virtual Teams Share Knowledge: Media Richness, Cultural Difference and Language Commonality." *Journal of World Business*, Vol. 48, No. 3, pp. 398-406.

8. Tenzer H., and Pudelko M. (2016) "Media Choice in Multilingual

Virtual Teams." *Journal of International Business Studies*, No 47, pp., 427--452.

9. Wadsworth M.B. and Blanchard A.L. (2015) "Influence Tactics in Virtual Teams." *Computers in Human Behavior*, Vol. 44, pp. 386-393.

10. Steizel S. and Rimbau-Gilabert E. (2013) "Upward Influence Tactics Through Technology Mediated Communication Tools." *Computers in Human Behavior*, Vol. 29, pp. 462-472.

11. Wadsworth M.B. and Blanchard A.L. (2015) "Influence Tactics in Virtual Teams." *Computers in Human Behavior*, Vol. 44, pp. 386-393.

12. Petersen D. "Lindred Greer: Why Virtual Teams Have More Conflict." www.gsb.stanford.edu/insights, November 7, 2014.

13. Hinds P.J. and Mortensen M. (2005) "Understanding Conflict in Geographically Distributed Teams: The Moderating Effects of Shared Identity, Shared Context, and Spontaneous Communication." *Organizational Science*, Vol. 16, No. 3.

14. Wakefield R.L., Leidner D.E. and Garrison G. (2008) "Research Note-A Model of Conflict, Leadership and Performance in Virtual Teams." *Information Systems Research*, Vol. 19, No. 4.

Index

integration into, 20
layers of, 21–22, 22*i*
*Culture and Organizations:
Software for the Mind*
(Hofstede), 20
culture shock, 22–23
curriculum vitae (CV), 41–42

D
data sharing, 153. *See also* knowledge sharing
decision-making
by email, 152–153
and leaders, physical absence
of, 9–10
reasons for, communication of,
135–136
technology for, 154–155
Denmark, communication style
of, 157
destroyers, virtual teams as, 25
details vs big picture, 40, 40*i*
developmental support (career),
56–57, 127–129
dialogue
about psychological safety, 84
communication type, 152
on conflict, 168
for cultural competence, 67–68
Diffuse cultures, 41–42

discrimination, 140
Discrimination and Fairness Paradigm, 140
distance
perceived, 136–139
psychological, 48–49, 137, 156
DiStefano, Joseph, 25
diversity (inclusion), 139–142
Diversity and Work Perspectives,
140–141
documentation, for clear communication, 157–158
duality, and cultural identity,
48–49
Dubé, Line, 148
dynamics, team, 4–5

E
Edmundson, Amy, 82–83
Ely, Robin J., 140–142
email
and after-hour use, 132
communication styles in,
33–34
cultural diversity in, 67,
157–158
emoticons in, 150, 163
etiquette, 100
influence and, 163

Index

Made in the USA
Las Vegas, NV
01 May 2023

71394907R00132